BETTER, FASTER EMAIL

BETTER, FASTER EMAIL

Getting the most
out of email

Joan Tunstall

ALLEN & UNWIN

First published in 1999 by
Allen & Unwin
9 Atchison Street, St Leonards 1590
Australia
Phone: (61 2) 8425 0100
Fax: (61 2) 9906 2218
E-mail: frontdesk@allen-unwin.com.au
Web: http://www.allen-unwin.com.au

National Library of Australia
Cataloguing-in-Publication entry:

Tunstall, Joan.
   Better, faster email: getting the most out of email.

   ISBN 1 86448 899 9.

   1. Electronic mail systems. 2. Written communication. I. Title.

384.34

Set in 11/13 pt Adobe Garamond by DOCUPRO, Sydney
Printed by Australian Print Group, Maryborough, Victoria

10 9 8 7 6 5 4 3 2 1

Contents

Figures

Acknowledgments

Thank you to the many people with whom I have corresponded by email, both for business and pleasure, especially to those who have contributed to the experiences told throughout this book. With you I learned to understand the joys of email communication.

Special thanks to Alex Spitzer for his knowledgeable and helpful comments on the manuscript, to my husband Ian who encouraged me to write, and to the Allen & Unwin team who have seen the job through to completion.

Screen images from Microsoft Outlook Express have been used to illustrate features offered by modern email software. These illustrations are reproduced with the permission of Microsoft Corporation. Outlook is a trademark of Microsoft Corporation in the United States and other countries.

chapter 1

How is email communication different?

Knowing how to use email effectively is an essential skill in business today. It is already widely used in the corporate world and more people are joining in each day.

Email is popular because it's so quick, easy and cost-effective. You may protest that email isn't quick or easy for you. You may find it a burden because every day there is a large amount of mail to handle, much of which is irrelevant, trivial or contains more information than you need for your job. You may dislike email because you don't like writing and would rather go back to the days when things were handled on the telephone.

Cheer up—with some simple organisational and writing skills you can overcome the email burden, turning it into a powerful tool to help you in your work. Even if you are slow at typing or get too many messages, it can still be a great way to get your job done. All it takes is an understanding of how to get the best out of email and how to overcome its worst features.

Yes, it is possible to get on top of your email and enjoy it. This book shows you how.

THE EMAIL DIFFERENCE

Email holds a unique position somewhere between a telephone conversation and an old-fashioned paper memo. You need to understand this position, its potential and its pitfalls, if you are to use email to best effect.

A telephone conversation

A telephone conversation is a direct two-way communication method that can be easily expanded to incorporate new information as required.

■ A telephone conversation

'Jane, can you give me an up-to-date price on powder granules?'
'Loose or packaged?'
'Packaged. I think they come in 10 kilo bags.'
'Yes, that's right. I only have last month's price. Will that do?'
'That's OK.'
'$106 for 10 kilos. $200 for 20 kilos. I can give a better price on larger quantities.'

While a telephone conversation lacks the visual clues of face-to-face communication, your tone of voice gives audio clues to the listener that help to convey your meaning. For example, 'That's OK' said quickly and cheerfully conveys agreement. If it was said more slowly and with a different inflection it could convey 'That's OK, I *guess*. I really wanted an up-to-date price, but I don't want to put you out too much', and the earlier conversation is likely to have run more like this:

■ Audio clues change the conversation

'That's OK,' said in a tone that indicates some reluctance.
'I'll give you these prices now but will do my best to get the

latest to you this afternoon. $106 for 10 kilos. $200 for 20 kilos.'

When you are talking on the telephone, you are likely to do some friendly chatting as the main business is being transacted. This chatting helps you to build relationships with the people you are dealing with as well as getting on with your work. It makes work more fun.

However, telephone conversations have limitations. There is the troublesome telephone tag where you keep missing each other and have to call back. Conversations also leave nothing for the formal record.

▨ The previous conversation left nothing for the record

'What do you mean, packaged granules are $120 for 10 kilos? I rang the other day and you told me $106.'
'That was the old price. They've gone up.'
'I did a quote on the basis of that conversation!'

A memo or letter

Memos or letters take more time and effort to handle, both on your part and the recipient's part. The onus is on you to make the information clear, so that it's understood the first time without the need for additional to-and-fro.

▨ A memo

To: Jane Gleeson
From: John Marks
Date: 16 June 1998
Subject: Price for Powder Granules
Jane,
Can you please give me the current price for 10 kilogram packages of powder granules? This will be used in a customer

quote to be submitted on 18 June 1998 and must remain firm
for up to 30 days.
Regards,
John

While the strictly formal language of the past has given
way to a friendlier, less stilted style in business, memos are
still structured and precise. People know that letters and
memos have a permanence, and no one wants to go on record
as being frivolous and unclear.

An advantage is that, unlike a two-way telephone conversation, business documents can be addressed to more than
one person. However, they still tend to be sent to a limited
audience.

One significant consideration is that letters and
memos involve delay. There is not only the time needed
for you to prepare them, but also the delivery time, the
time for the recipients to respond and another lot of delivery
time.

Today, because of the effort involved, letters and memos
tend to be restricted to important matters, situations where
a paper record is required, or where longer documents require
deliberation.

An email message

You will find that email has characteristics of both voice and
paper communication. For example, email messages are often
friendly and conversational, so they have some of the warmth
of telephone interactions.

▦ An email message

Hi Jane,
Can you give me the current price for packaged powder
granules? I want the 10 kilo pack.

Cheers, John
PS Hope the dinner went well last night.

Email messages are like letters, because they give you time to think through the issues and to change things so that you're sure they are right. However, because email messages are used for a wide range of interactions they are typically prepared more quickly than a letter. Fortunately, if you have missed something, the fast delivery and turnaround allows clarification when necessary.

An email reply

Hello John,
The dinner went really well. I didn't even burn the food.
$106 for 10 kilos. Larger packs are cheaper. This is last month's price—does that matter?
Regards,
Jane

Return email

Last month's price is OK provided it's good for 30 days. Pls confirm.
John

Because email messages can be saved and printed, they have similar permanence to ordinary paper records. This makes them ideal for fast business communication.

An extra plus is that, while email messages have the conversational benefit of telephone dialogue, they avoid telephone tag. The two parties don't have to be working at the same time. You can respond when you are available and according to your own schedule.

However, one problem is the lack of audio clues, which can lead to misunderstandings. It is especially so because email responses tend to be dashed off without taking the same care as for a letter and are often used to communicate things that would never be put in a letter.

A major difference and benefit of email is that it's easy to send a message to a lot of people at once. However, you will find this ease of distribution is also the greatest curse of email. When email messages are sent to large groups of people, many of whom have only limited interest in the content, the result is junk email and email overload.

USE EMAIL FOR . . .

Basically, you can assume that email is good for all forms of business communication provided you consider the simple precautions and exceptions given later in this chapter. Here are some things email is especially good for.

Messages for a lot of people

Email is great for sending messages to a lot of people simultaneously. A message can go out to 50 or more people without wasting time at the office photocopier, and large attached documents can be distributed without the cost of paper and printing.

Messages you need to get out quickly

If your message has to get out quickly, email is again ideal. Be aware, however, that many people process their email only once a day, so if the message has to be read in less than 24 hours, you should telephone or use some other means, such as an urgent facsimile. Some corporate email systems allow you to check if people within the company have read a message you have sent.

Messages for fast turnaround in different time zones

If you need to reach people on the other side of the world, then email is a great help. You can send your message during your working day and the recipient can respond during their working day. When you arrive the next morning, a response is available and you didn't have to get up in the middle of the night to make a telephone call.

> *When I'm late sending notice of a meeting and the deadline is getting close, I look to see who's opened my email message and ring those who haven't. It's quicker than ringing everyone.*
>
> *—Emily, Executive Assistant*

DON'T USE EMAIL FOR . . .

There are a few situations where you should definitely not use email and others where you need to be careful.

Long and complicated messages

Email messages are generally read on the screen and not printed. Also, most recipients want to process each item quickly. Therefore, email is generally not good for long, complicated messages.

On the other hand, environmentally conscious companies may have policies for using electronic documents rather than paper, so you may *have* to use email for long messages. If you have to send a lot of information in a message, structure it in such a way that the reader can scan it quickly and process the detail later.

Questions that require a lot of clarification

With email the onus is on you to present information clearly so that it can be understood and answered without undue to-and-fro. If you don't have enough information to ask your question clearly, the result can be a lot of clarifying messages going back and forth. You are better off picking up the telephone to ask your questions. It will save time for everyone.

Indiscreet messages

Email messages can be saved, printed and sent on. You should think of them as having the same permanence as a letter, even though their informality may tempt you to think otherwise. Never use indiscreet language or content in an email message. Don't use email to bad-mouth the boss to a friend. Don't use email to conduct a steamy love affair.

> We had an incident when somebody unwittingly copied their love note to the entire office.
>
> —Barry, Business Analyst

Would you want what you have written to be posted on every office noticeboard? The speed and ease of email communication can result in something equivalent to just that, and the possibilities for embarrassment from human errors are enormous. Even without mistakes, the ease of passing on messages means email can fly like office gossip. You should assume that any email message you write could end up in the inbox of the person you would least like to receive it. If you wouldn't like that person to get it, then don't send it!

Confidential messages

If an email message contains confidential information, exercise care in sending it. If the information you want to send is highly confidential, you are better to put it in a letter or memo marked as confidential.

You should assume at all times that email is not a secure form of transmission. Messages can sometimes be read by other people and there is also the problem of them being passed on, perhaps to inappropriate people.

Angry exchanges

It is impossible to take back angry words once they have been spoken. In a telephone or face-to-face confrontation these angry words hurt, but their recollection is only on the part of the participants and tends to soften with time. When those angry words are written, they stay in their stark reality, to be mulled over, read by others and used against you, causing their hurt over and over again.

> I simply write, 'Disagree. We should discuss face-to-face.'
> —Kate, Business Manager

It is most unlikely that you would express your anger in an official letter. People are generally not that foolish. The immediacy of email can trap you into responding in a conversational way. If someone sends something hurtful, the natural response is to rebuke the hurt straight away, just as would happen if the person said the offending thing to your face.

If you are angry, never use email. Wait until you have simmered down. Even if your email system lets you delete a message after you have sent it, don't risk it; the person may read it before you have second thoughts. Don't even write a heated response and plan to sit on it for a day before mailing it, as it's easy for messages sitting in your outbox to be mailed inadvertently.

Messages that should not be in written form

The written word, without visual or audio clues, is easily misinterpreted. You may inadvertently cause offence. Some

> *I sent an email message which was misunderstood. I was surprised and shocked by the message I received in return. Within a day I had sent off an equally biting response to even the score.*
>
> *Afterwards I realised the foolishness of my behaviour and initiated a face-to-face conversation which put an end to the nasty-grams. However, this was not before my boss, who had been copied on the messages, saw fit to reprimand me and before other more senior managers had seen the exchange.*
>
> —*Joshua, Office Worker*

things should never be written. If you are writing something that is emotional, that requires tone of voice or conversational feedback to soften the words, don't write it. If you are writing something that could be easily misinterpreted, don't write it.

If you decide the message should be written, then draft it carefully. Give it time before you write it and, most importantly, put yourself in the other person's position. How will they receive the message? Will they be able to interpret your intent clearly?

It may be a good idea to ask a colleague to take a look at what you have written before it is sent. A word of caution, though: don't let someone else encourage you into intemperate behaviour. It will be your name on the message and you that suffers the consequences. As a guide, if your message is too sensitive or inflammatory to be put in a letter, then don't put it in an email message.

Hiding from direct contact with people

Another related matter is using email to send a message that you find unpleasant or difficult to say in person. Some workers are reporting that their managers use email to bully and intimidate them. Hiding behind email is clearly unacceptable. Don't be weak by using email when the right thing to do is to talk to the person.

BEFORE SENDING AN EMAIL MESSAGE

As a final precaution, before you send an email message apply these two simple rules.

1. See your message through the reader's eyes

Read your message again, this time through your reader's eyes. Think about things like:

- Was it easy to read?
- Did I think it was junk mail?
- Have I just been annoyed or offended?
- Was the message in the right tone for me?

2. Think twice before sending an email message

Now, just one more time before you hit the send button, ask yourself whether you should be sending it.

- Does the message suit email?
- Are you angry?
- Should you use a letter, a telephone call or visit the person instead?

ABOUT MAILERS

The *mailer* is the computer program that you use to send, receive and organise your email messages. This is also commonly called an *email client* or *email application*.

Throughout this book it has been assumed that you already use email and know your way around the mailer you use. If this isn't the case, in the appendix there are some basic instructions on what you need to know. However, for information specific to your system you will need help from the online help, a manual, or a person in your office who knows how your mailer works.

Just a few years ago, mailers provided only simple text messaging and were driven by typed commands. They were quite hard to use. This has changed. Today's mailers are sophisticated windows-oriented programs with point-and-click organisation tools that are very easy to use. If you have a recent release of popular email software, you will have an easy-to-use mailer with all the new features designed to enhance office efficiency. Unfortunately, if you are still working with a simple text messaging system there will be things that can't be done with your system.

The mailer you use may be somewhere between the two, particularly if you work in a large organisation. Changing the email software involves disruption and the retraining of users. It's therefore not a simple matter for big companies to keep up with the latest releases.

HOW EMAIL CAN MAKE A DIFFERENCE TO YOUR WORK

You may be in a small business where most of your messages are to outside clients and potential customers, or you may be in a large organisation where you mainly use email to contact other people in your company. Regardless of the size of your organisation, you will find that email can help you to do your job better.

Here are some of the ways people use email, the skills they have developed for organising themselves and how they use the tools provided with their mailers.

Email connects you to people and information

When your job is to keep people informed, then you can get your messages out more effectively with email.

The job is even easier when you have the addresses of the people you want to contact readily on hand. One of your most valuable email tools is your address book, which puts your distribution lists, and addresses of business associates and friends, at your fingertips.

People also find email is a great way to contact others when they need help. Without email, you ask or ring your favourite contacts, who hopefully know the answer or can refer you to someone else who does. Email provides you with another approach.

Most large companies set up email mailing groups or shared folders for people with similar interests—salespeople, engineers, investment advisers and such like. These are a very useful way to share information among a team of people. (Chapter 3 provides information on address books, mailing groups and shared folders, as well as guidance on sending email messages to the right people.)

> *I used to wait until I had enough to print a full marketing bulletin. Today I email hot information straight away. The less important stuff I still hold and consolidate into a single email bulletin. This way people get what they need quickly but I don't overload their inboxes.*
>
> —*Simon, Product Manager*

> *When I can't figure something out and my local contacts can't help, I send an email message to the mailing group of all analysts in our offices around the world. There's usually someone out there who has an answer or who can suggest something for me to try.*
>
> —*Rebecca, Computer Analyst*

Email can help you to manage your time better

In an old-fashioned office, people are constantly taking telephone calls and talking to people who have popped by just to ask a quick question. It takes a lot of discipline on your part to manage these interruptions, to keep them short and to keep your concentration on higher-priority tasks.

> *Some guys I work with leave all their messages in the inbox. That's crazy! They can't work out which ones still need action and what is dead.*
>
> —*Amanda, Administrative Assistant*

When these people change to using email, you are able to process their messages with a block of your time, rather than having to contend with them as annoying interruptions. This helps you to manage your time better.

You can also save yourself heaps of time every day by organising your messages with your email filing system. With a little bit of thought, you can plan an email filing system that suits the information you are handling and the way you like to work. You can even file messages automatically if your mailer has filtering capability. Knowing how to use filing and filtering tools efficiently is an important email skill. (Chapter 4 has ideas for organising your email messages, and information about filing and filtering. It also has some simple time management hints for managing email overload.)

> *I have trouble tracking down information I take over the telephone, since I usually write it down on the first loose piece of paper I can find on my desk. With most people now using email, I've mostly solved the problem.*
>
> —*Craig, Project Officer*
>
> ---
>
> *Because I know the messages are going to be easy to find later, I just skip-read them and file them. It saves me time when the messages come in. I only give them full attention when I'm ready to use them.*
>
> —*Fernando, Information Analyst*

Email helps you to keep better records

Email often replaces spoken conversations, as well as letters and memos. This puts the information all in one place so that it's easier to manage.

Using the search capabilities of email, the hunt for a particular message is as simple as typing a few key words and letting the computer do the work. It will sift out the messages that meet your criteria. (Chapter 5 has information on using email messages for the record, how to find them, which ones to keep, which ones to delete and how to go about cleaning up old messages. Chapter 6 has some special warnings about the privacy of your messages and the way your messages can continue to exist even after you have deleted them.)

Email helps you to work with other people better

Collaborating on a project can be a difficult experience when people are in different companies, locations or time zones. Email helps to take the pain out of collaboration. Documents, even quite lengthy ones, can be sent quickly to all members of the group. Alternatively, you can pass a document to one person for comment who can add his or her changes and forward it to the next person.

Here's a tip that might help you. When everyone in the group is using the same email system, you may be able to specify the order in which people are to receive documents. Note, however, that you need to think about the routing getting stuck with a person who is away. The mailer may report back to the originator each time the message is passed on, so that you know when this has happened. (If you are having trouble sending documents via email, look at the suggestions in Chapter 7.)

> *I belong to an international marketing team. We use email to pass around sales presentations and to get feedback quickly. This gets an international perspective into the material up-front and saves me having to rework the material for my country later.*
>
> —*Julia, Marketing Manager*

You can connect to the world with email

When your email system is connected to the Internet, it's possible to reach beyond the walls of your company to

> *I teach an evening class in calligraphy. Through the calligraphy mailing list I have asked other people how they overcome difficulties, such as teaching left-handed students.*
>
> —*Esperanza, Arts Coordinator*

like-minded people throughout the world. There are thousands of worldwide mailing lists grouping together people with interests as diverse as archiving and zoology. You may be able to find a group relating to your professional or personal interests.

Posting a single email message to an Internet mailing list reaches everyone who has subscribed to the list. This may be just a handful, or thousands of people.

> *Our son, who's at university, never phones. But since we got our email address, we often hear from him. He just fires off a message when he's logged on doing other work.*
>
> —*Emma, Parent*

With all your work to be done, don't forget that email is a friendly way to communicate. You can send an interesting snippet or a scanned photograph with a few keystrokes, when a telephone call may end up as a long chat and a letter may never get sent. (Chapter 8 includes some basic Internet jargon, as well as other useful ideas. Chapter 9 shows you how to find and join Internet mailing lists.)

Email can be integrated with other office systems

In some companies, other office systems—such as personal calendars, document management systems and work-flow software—are integrated with email.

Monthly accounts, performance statistics, quality measurements and such like are accumulated and reported by computer programs. With some types of computer programs it's possible to add an extra step so that it also sends email messages to selected people.

This ability for other office products to integrate with email is generally a feature offered by those products rather than your mailer and is therefore outside the scope of this book. However, it's certainly worth investigating what can be done at your office so that email becomes an even more powerful tool for getting your work done.

> *I find the combination of email with the schedular is a powerful tool for arranging meetings, booking rooms and such. Moving a meeting to a different time automatically sends an email notification of the change to all the members.*
>
> —Paul, Administrative Assistant

> *I get an email message from the computer when the monthly summary is done, so that I can start work on it as soon as it's ready. It helps me to get on top of issues more quickly so that I can advise the management team.*
>
> —Aaron, Financial Manager

ON BECOMING A POWERFUL EMAIL USER

Does the observation below made by a business executive have possible implications for you?

This suggests that the next chapter, 'How Can I Write Better Email Messages?', could be important to your future success. The chapter shows you how to write email messages clearly and quickly. You will also learn effective approaches to use with messages for external customers and clients.

> *I've noticed that as email has become more entrenched, the people that use email effectively tend to wield more influence than those who write badly or annoy people with their messages.*
>
> —Sarah, Business Executive

KEY POINTS

- Email messages are like telephone conversations because they:
  — Are friendly and conversational.
  — Are delivered quickly, so clarification is easy.
- Email messages are like letters or memos because they:
  — Are written and don't have audio clues.
  — Give you time to think and to change the content.
  — Can be saved and printed to be an official business record.
  — Don't require the two parties to be communicating at the same time.

  Email is also:
  — Easily distributed to a large number of people simultaneously.
  — Easily passed on to other people.
- You can use email for most business messages.
- Don't use email for:
  — Complicated messages or questions that need a lot of clarification.
  — Confidential, sensitive, indiscreet or angry messages.
  — Hiding from direct contact with people.
- Email can help you to:
  — Connect with people and information.
  — Manage your time better.
  — Keep better records.
  — Collaborate easily and make more friends.

EXERCISES

The exercises in this book are designed for you to put into practice some of the ideas presented in each chapter. You are usually asked to review things you actually do at work, so that you learn from your own business activities.

On this occasion, the exercise is a self-evaluation quiz. This quiz is a quick way for you to review how you currently use email and to give you an early insight into things you might do in order to become a more effective email user.

Read each question and, in the list that follows the question, tick the boxes which apply to you. You may tick more than one box per question. If you tick the last box in the list you seem to be in control of that aspect using email. If you have ticked one of the other boxes in the list, you will find information that will help you to learn more in the chapter(s) indicated.

1. **Are you writing effective messages?**
   - ☐ I think my writing is too slow and I spend a lot of time trying to get my message right.
   - ☐ My email messages seem to be a lot of chit-chat.
   - ☐ I seem to type the same answer over and over again for different people.
   - ☐ People aren't answering my email messages.
   - ☐ I sometimes send private messages. I'm not sure this is a safe thing to do.
   - ☐ None of the above—I am writing appropriate messages that achieve the desired responses.

   To learn how to write concise email messages that get your message across, turn to Chapter 2. To understand more about email privacy, read Chapter 6.

2. **Are your email messages well organised?**
   - ☐ I get more messages than I can handle.
   - ☐ I don't use folders yet. Perhaps I should.

☐ I think my folders could be arranged better.

☐ I don't know how to search for a message I want.

☐ I don't know how to use filters to automatically file my mail.

☐ My folders need a good clean-out, but I'm not sure how to go about it.

☐ I'm confused about which messages I should keep or file elsewhere.

☐ None of the above—my filing system works well for me.

Read Chapter 4 to learn how to organise your messages for faster processing. Chapter 5 has ideas on how to find, archive and clean up your messages.

3. **Is email being used well for disseminating information?**

☐ I think other people are sending me unnecessary information.

☐ I'm getting junk messages from people I don't know.

☐ I'm not sure who I should copy on my mail—the rules seem to have changed.

☐ I would like to use email to update people, but I'm concerned I may be overloading them.

☐ None of the above—I receive and send just the right amount of information.

Chapter 3 gives some guidelines on who to send email messages to, so that you enhance communication rather than clog it. Chapter 4 has information on handling unwanted mail.

4. **Is email being used to conduct business outside your company effectively?**

☐ I don't know how to send email messages to people in other companies.

☐ I'm concerned about the image of our company that we are presenting through email. I could do with some tips.

☐ I would like to send my customers email messages, but they are having trouble reading the documents I send.

☐ I can't read some of the documents clients send me.

☐ None of the above—we conduct our external business well with email, or we don't use email with outside people.

Chapter 2 explains how to write clear business email messages for both internal and external customers. Chapter 7 offers some help in understanding incompatibilities between different computer systems.

5. **Is email giving you better control over your schedule?**

☐ Handling email interrupts my normal work.

☐ I'm spending more time each day processing my mail.

☐ I'm not sure if I have to reply to all my mail. It would save time if I didn't.

☐ Email always seems to take priority. I don't think it should.

☐ None of the above—email is helping me to schedule my work better.

Chapter 4 has some time management tips that will help you to set your priorities.

6. **Do you know how to contact people easily via email?**

☐ I don't know how to send a question to a group of my peers.

☐ I have no idea whether shared folders exist on our system.

☐ I don't use my email address book.

☐ None of the above—I know my contact addresses and have them organised.

Chapter 3 has information on addressing and mail groups.

chapter 2

How can I write better email messages?

Would you like to write good email messages? A good email message is readily understood. It will be read and actioned properly. It will take you little time to write and will take the recipient little time to read.

This chapter describes time-saving techniques for writing your messages faster. You will learn how to help people process your email messages more easily, and you will learn clear writing techniques to apply to your messages.

THE STRUCTURE OF AN EMAIL MESSAGE

This first section briefly defines the components of an email message as used in this book. Even though your mailer may look different and may name things differently, you should be able to find the standard elements shown in Figure 2.1.

There may be extra elements displayed with your messages, such as details of the computers that the message has passed through. This information (which is only really useful for technicians wanting to track problems) is sometimes displayed in the header information or at the end of the message.

Figure 2.1 The elements of an email message

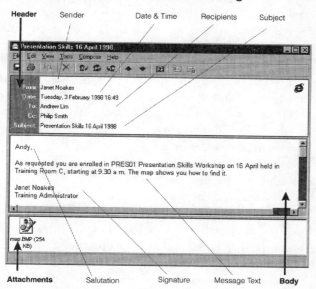

Header. The header contains addressing and delivery information and the subject of the message.

Sender. The sender is the address of the person who sent the message. If you sent the message, your address will appear here. Some mailers display the name from the comment field of an Internet address, rather than the email address, as is the case in the illustration. (See Chapter 3 for an explanation of Internet addresses.)

Recipient(s). The recipient is the name or address of the person to whom the message has been sent. If you received the message, your name or address will appear here. There may be more than one recipient. There may also be copied recipients. (Chapter 3 has more on recipients.)

Date and time. The date and time is automatically inserted when a message is sent. Some mailers display the time in the zone where the mail was sent; others convert it to your time zone.

Subject. The subject is a short description of the main point of the message. It is provided by the sender. When you reply to a message, or forward a message, 'Re:' or 'Fwd:' usually appears automatically in front of the original subject line.

Body. The body contains the email message. Just like the body of a letter, the body of an email message has a salutation, the message text and a signature. When this message is in response to an earlier message, the body may also contain a copy of the original message and other messages that have been sent in reply to the original.

Salutation. The salutation is a greeting to the recipient at the beginning of the message.

Message text. The message text is the actual message.

Signature. The signature signs off the message.

Attachments. Attachments are documents enclosed within the email message. Usually the icons for the attached documents and the names of these documents are displayed, but not the actual contents of the documents. Some mailers display attachments as garbled characters at the end of the message body. Others simply list the names of the attachments in the header information. (Chapter 7 has more on attachments.)

COMPOSING EMAIL MESSAGES FASTER

When you have more email messages than you can handle, one way of getting through them is to answer the mail faster. Read on for a few tips on writing email messages quickly.

Keep your message short

The most obvious way to save time is to keep your messages short. Don't feel as if you have to tell a story with every message. It's perfectly acceptable to respond with one line, or one word if that is enough. 'Agreed' may be all that's needed.

Later in this chapter you will be shown techniques for writing short, clear messages that get straight to the point.

Reduce your keystrokes

Apart from keeping the message short, here are other ways to reduce the amount of typing you have to do:

* Omit the salutation.
* Leave out friendly introductory and closing flourishes like 'Thank you for your reply' and 'I hope this meets your needs'.
* Don't respond to chit-chat. People often include it to show they have thought of you personally. They don't really need a reply and won't consider you rude when you don't respond to it.
* Don't start your own chit-chat. It is sometimes a useful device to build relationships. Use it when you need it, and leave it out otherwise.
* Use abbreviations for frequently used words and phrases but only when you know they will be clearly understood by the reader (see Chapter 8).
* Use an automatic signature (see Chapter 8) or omit your signature.
* Learn the shortcut or key commands for any tools you use frequently, such as the spelling checker and address book look-up.
* Use form letters and forms for messages that you reuse frequently (see below).

Practise

Believe in your own competence. Stop tinkering with the words over and over again trying to get them perfect. If you have applied clear writing techniques from the outset, your message should need little revision.

Working intensively at applying clear writing techniques for just a few weeks will improve your habitual reactions. Soon you will be able to communicate effectively in the first draft for most messages.

USING FORM LETTERS

If you find yourself typing the same response over and over again, create a *form letter* instead. With a form letter you will only have to type the words specific to the situation.

Form letters are also known as *templates* or *stationery*. See if your mailer has one of these options. If it has, type your form letter and save it using the instructions specific to your mailer. If these options aren't available, you can still use form letters. Start a new message and type your form letter, as in Figure 2.2, then save the message as a draft or send it to yourself.

When you are ready to send the message, you begin with the form letter and change it to make the specific message you want to send. Do the following:

1. Open a new message using the desired template, stationery or draft message. The form letter is displayed.
2. Make your changes to the text of the form letter.
3. Send the message.

You will want to keep an unchanged version of the form letter. Some mailers won't do this when you use the procedure set out above. In that case, use the steps below. Also use these steps if your form letter was saved as a message sent to yourself:

1. Open the message that contains the desired form letter.
2. Copy the text of the form letter to the clipboard.
3. Open a new message.
4. Paste the text of the form letter into the message.

Figure 2.2 A form letter

Change these

5. Make your changes to the text of the form letter.
6. Send the message.

USING FORMS

A few mailers also have the ability to create and use forms. Email forms help in the same way as paper forms do: they provide spaces for the respondent to fill in so that they supply the information you want. Forms can be a quick and helpful way to get accurate and complete information. For example, you might have forms for recording monthly sales statistics, completing a weekly timesheet, submitting an error report or putting in a leave request.

You create the form using the design tools provided with your mailer. With a corporate email system the form may then be stored in a central location where people can access it when they need it. Alternatively, the form can be sent to a person who can use it as a template. When people need to use the form, say to submit their weekly timesheet, they do the following:

1. Open a new message using the desired form. The form is displayed in the body of the email message.
2. Fill in the blanks on the form.
3. Send the email message.

Unlike many other email facilities, forms can be used only by people who have the same type of mailer as you. If you send a form to someone with a different type of mailer, it will be indecipherable.

DOING BUSINESS BY EMAIL

When you are doing business with someone outside your company, you are conveying an impression of your company. You must take as much care as if you were writing a letter on your company letterhead.

Use an email letterhead

A lot of people use their company email address for personal communication outside of their company. So when you are transacting business on behalf of your company and not for yourself, you may need to make this understood.

A way to do this is to devise a simple letterhead with the company name. Keep it to just a few lines, because this shows at the top of the message and lengthens your message. If you make a long letterhead, the reader will see nothing but the letterhead at first glance and you would rather they saw some of your message as well.

You don't need to put the street address and other contact information in the letterhead. Include this in the signature rather than cluttering the front of the message.

You can use things like colour, italics and bold. Just remember that some businesses will have mailers that display these as plain text characters only. Make a letterhead that will still look acceptable when this happens. The example below will work. Save your letterhead as a form letter so that you don't have to type it each time.

▨ A simple company letterhead

~~~~~~~~~~~~~~~~~~~~~~~~~~~~~~~~
AAA Company International
A.C.N. 000 000 000
~~~~~~~~~~~~~~~~~~~~~~~~~~~~~~~~

Some mailers also have an HTML stationery option which allows you to create letterheads with sophisticated colour graphics. The problem is, your recipient may not have a mailer that can display your fancy work. It will also make the message much longer, and hence slower to receive and bigger to save. This will become less of a problem over time when more people are using modern software, have faster links and more free disk space. At present it's safer to assume they don't have these things. (Chapter 8 explains HTML stationery.)

Choose the right salutation

Messages to your colleagues and friends will be on a first name basis. In business it's usually acceptable to use a person's first name, but you are more likely to write 'Dear Stephen' than just 'Stephen' or 'Steve'.

If you feel the situation demands formality, then use the person's title and last name—'Dear Ms Winterburn'. You can easily change to using the person's first name if they respond to you in an informal way. When you are dealing internationally it's better to err on the side of formality.

Rather than writing something like 'Dear Sir/Madam' or 'Dear Colleague', simply omit the salutation. This is quite acceptable.

Use an expanded signature

Use your signature to complete the extra details that are usually included on the letterhead. If you have an Internet World Wide Web site, remember to put this in too. Modern mailers will make this a hot link, so readers only have to click on it and their Web browser will go to your Web site.

▦ A business signature

Danielle Webster
Sales Manager

AAA Company International
16 Wealth Street, Melbourne
Ph 03 0000 0000
http://www.aaaint.com.au

A recent innovation in mailers is the vCard facility which allows you to attach business card details to your email message (see Chapter 8).

Make it personal

When you are writing to a person for the first time, it's a courtesy to tell them where you obtained their email address—from their World Wide Web page, a business publication, referral from an associate or whatever.

Many people these days get huge volumes of unsolicited commercial email. This has been named spam and most people instantly delete it. (Read more about spam in Chapter 4.) You don't want your genuine letter to be treated as spam. Nor do you want to be a perpetrator of spam. Your letter should appear as a personal communication, not as a high-volume form letter.

GETTING PEOPLE TO READ YOUR MESSAGES

Are you having trouble getting people to read and respond to your messages? It's best to look at yourself as the possible cause before you start blaming others.

Write better messages

Start by reviewing the messages you are sending to see if they are communicating clearly. Getting the following things right will greatly improve your chances of an appropriate response:

- Use an informative subject line which will entice the recipients to open the message.
- Keep your message short so that it isn't a drudge to read.
- Put the main point at the top of the message.
- State what action you want, by whom and by when.
- Send the mail to people who can respond with the action you want.

Make it easier to reply

You will also have more success if you make your messages easier to reply to. Here are some ideas for doing this:

- Insert numbers in front of your questions to make it easier for readers to reply. They then just have to type the question number and their answer.
- Number the paragraphs and subparagraphs of long messages. This also helps for draft documents, where people

are expected to respond with changes to selected paragraphs.

Be a nicer person

Remember that people like to work with friendly colleagues. Does this friendly person show in your messages, or are you making the mistake of being pompous and demanding? Developing a friendly conversational writing style will definitely benefit your working relationships.

Also realise that if you are slow at responding to your email, then others may be doing the same to you in return. Sharpen your own act if you expect others to do likewise.

Use 'Urgent' when it's needed

Genuinely urgent matters can be highlighted in two ways:

- You can usually set the priority of your message before sending it. An urgent message is put at the top of the recipient's inbox where it's more likely to be viewed or it may be highlighted in some way on the recipient's screen.
- Putting the word 'Urgent' in the subject also works as a good attention grabber.

Make sure it *is* urgent. Consider whether the recipients are going to feel duped when they read the message and think you have overreacted. Explain why you need their attention in a hurry. It may not be self-evident.

Almost everything you work on is important. However, in most situations few matters are so genuinely urgent as to need others to drop what they are doing to attend to your need immediately. When people get the idea that everything you send is marked 'Urgent', they start ignoring it and you have lost the power of a very valuable device.

Ask why your mail is being ignored

It may help to ask some friendly associates why they are ignoring your mail. They may be able to help you with something you haven't seen for yourself. Then, after you have fixed any problems you may be causing, it's safe to consider whether the fault may lie elsewhere.

Maybe you are having a problem with just one or two people. Ask if others are having the same trouble. The slow responders could be disorganised or overloaded, in which case you could consider reverting to the telephone and paper mail for these people. This may help if they are technophobic and avoiding their computer, but with disorganised people it won't work any better.

To protect yourself you could use the feature that lets you know when they have received and opened your mail. When there is no action for a reasonable time, follow up by telephone.

When all else fails and the delays are affecting your work, discuss the problem with your manager. It's not advisable to start an email war on this matter. You'll get better results by talking it over sensibly.

LAYING OUT YOUR MESSAGE

You will want your message to look as good as possible when it's received by the other person and for it to be easy for them to understand. Giving some consideration to layout and punctuation can help you to achieve this.

Keep lines short

When you are typing your message it will usually word-wrap the lines on your screen rather than you having to press 'Enter' or 'Return' at the end of each line. However, when your message is received it may no longer word-wrap and if the recipient's screen has shorter lines than yours, your message will look untidy. The example shows a paragraph as it could look on your screen and how it may end up being displayed on the recipient's screen.

Paragraph with word-wrap

This is a paragraph of text to demonstrate what can
happen when the message is displayed by another
mailer with shorter lines than yours.

Same paragraph without word-wrap and with shorter lines

This is a paragraph of text to demonstrate
what can
happen when the message is displayed by
another
mailer with shorter lines than yours.

The way to give your messages the best chance of looking good is to use relatively short lines. You can do this by reducing the size of your message window when you type the message, or you may be able to specify the number of characters per line.

A line length of about 70 characters will display well on most screens. It also leaves room for your message to be indented when it is quoted in replies and still display properly.

Use simple layout effects

Use spacing and headings in long messages to make them easier to understand and help the readers to scan more quickly. You might like to use bold, italic and colour as well, but the problem is that these may not appear on the recipient's screen. Only use them when you are sure they can be viewed.

If you are writing to a person in your own company or someone with a modern mailer, then they will probably display.

Use upper and lower case

In email culture, words in CAPITALS are SHOUTING, so use them sparingly. It's considered very rude to shout for long. Quite apart from email culture, messages in capital letters are too hard to read. This is shown in the example below.

■ Don't use all upper case

NEVER WRITE YOUR WHOLE MESSAGE IN CAPITAL LETTERS. IT MAKES YOUR MESSAGE VERY HARD TO READ.

Don't use all lower case

the same can be said of email written all in lower case. this is also too hard to read.

Go steady on emphatic punctuation

Conversational speech has voice emphasis to support it. Unfortunately, the richness of this is missing from the written word. You can use punctuation as a quick way to change emphasis and meaning, as shown in the example below.

■ Emphasis changed by punctuation

Anton won again.   (Congratulations.)
Anton won again!   (This has to stop.)
Anton won again!@#! (I hate him.)

This is a device for casual notes only. In business emails, it's better to stick with standard punctuation, and to use exclamation marks sparingly.

Avoid smileys

The users of early email created a punctuation device called *smileys*. These use various character combinations to make facial expressions and convey emotion. A smiley looked at sideways makes a face, as in the examples below.

Some smileys

;-)	a wink or sly grin
:-(	sad or angry
8–0	shocked or amazed

Smileys are cheerful and some are very clever, but in general the business world doesn't understand or use them. To the untrained eye they look like spurious, messy punctuation, so you will probably have to give smileys a miss at work.

THE KEYS TO CLEAR EMAIL COMMUNICATION

For the most part, in business correspondence, you are going to have to depend on your carefully expressed, clear writing to get your message across.

Your primary objective should always be for your message to have only one possible meaning which is fully understood by your reader. Unclear communication can result in problems like unnecessary to-and-fro, recipients failing to act appropriately, missed opportunities and hurt feelings. A CLEAR email message will be:

Concise
Logical
Empathetic
Action-oriented
Right

Concise. A brief message in simple conversational language is faster for you to write and more pleasant for your readers to read.

Logical. A message in logical steps, remembering to include any context your readers need, will be more easily understood.

Empathetic. When you identify with your readers, your message will be written in the right tone and in words they will readily understand.

Action-oriented. When you remember to explain to your readers what you want them to do next, they are more likely to do it.

Right. A complete message, with no important facts missing, with all the facts right and with correct spelling, will save your readers having to return to you to clarify details.

WRITING CONCISELY

When you write concisely, your message is brief and to the point. While conciseness is important in any form of letter writing, it's even more so with email. Email messages are usually read on a computer screen, skimmed quickly and processed quickly. You have to grab your readers' attention and get them to act on your message. This is more likely to happen if it's short.

Get attention with your subject

Get your readers' attention right from the start with a short, informative subject. The subject should encapsulate the main point of your message in a few words. It will help your readers to know the purpose of your message without reading the message text.

An informative subject may make the difference between your message being read or passed over. And if it is passed over, at least you will have put your key point across. The example below shows some subjects which have been reworded to be more informative.

Uninformative	Informative
Planning meeting	Pls attend planning meeting 11 Jul 3 p.m.
Order #1546	Order #1546 has parts missing
Travel claims	Travel claims - 23 June is cut-off date
Engineering report	Tolerance figures for engineering report

The amount of the subject that is displayed on the recipient's screen varies. To give your message the best chance, keep it to around 30 characters and put the most important part at the beginning.

Use conversational language

There is nothing clever involved in writing concisely. It's as easy as writing the way you speak, in conversational language, using simple words and short sentences. It's the most natural way for you to write and makes for better understanding.

When writers try to be dignified they end up using longer sentences and uncommon words. The result is often unclear despite the extra effort. Pompous and trite phrases such as 'It will be recalled that' and 'It has come to my attention' sound dated in normal correspondence and even sillier in email messages. In conversation you would say 'Remember' and 'I've heard'. These read more easily as well.

The example below rewrites the text of an email announcement in conversational tone. Which would you rather receive?

Employee notice

Will all employees please note that henceforth car parking spaces are assigned to a particular person and must be used by only that person. Usage of another person's car space will not be tolerated.

Conversational version

From today car parking is allocated. Please help by only using the space assigned to you.

Here's a good test—read your messages aloud. If you hear yourself reading things that you would never say, then change them.

Write simple sentences

Your sentences should be short. However, you need to avoid the irritating bang-bang-bang of a lot of short sentences in sequence by varying the length occasionally. In the example below, joining a couple of sentences makes the paragraph flow more smoothly.

An email message with all short sentences

We can ship today. The boxes will arrive at 6 p.m. The signs will be delivered at 7 p.m. Can you keep the depot open late?

The message revised to flow more smoothly

We can ship today. The boxes will arrive at 6 p.m. and the signs at 7 p.m. Can you keep the depot open late?

People use variety naturally when they speak. You also need to use variety in your writing. Here's a rule of thumb. Long words of three or more syllables need short sentences. Shorter words can take longer sentences.

Use active speech

Try to use lively and interesting words. Your writing will also seem more lively and personal when you talk about people doing things rather than about things being done by people. The example below shows you the difference. It's not too hard to get this right. If you make the person the subject of your sentence, you will rarely make a mistake.

■ **Things being done by people**

The report was written by John.
A letter of thanks should be sent.

People doing things

John wrote the report.
You should send a letter of thanks.

GETTING YOUR MESSAGE TO FLOW LOGICALLY

Having chosen to read your message, your readers only want to read it once. If they have to go back to sort out what you are saying, then you have failed to write logically. The major source of the problem is mixing ideas together.

When you put more than one idea in a sentence or mix ideas within the same paragraph, you end up with fuzzy communication. This leads to confusion and misunderstandings. Look at the example below.

■ **A message with mixed ideas**

The trade show starts next Tuesday and runs until Friday. You are in charge of set-up. I have arranged for the equipment to be delivered to stand 8. You need to be there at 8.30 a.m. for the show and Monday.

The ideas in clear order

You are in charge of the trade show set-up next Monday. I have arranged for the equipment to be delivered to our stand (stand 8) at 8.30 a.m.

The show runs from Tuesday to Friday. You are needed for booth duty at 8.30 a.m. each of these days.

In the reworked example the set-up and booth duty responsibilities are much clearer because they are no longer muddled together. Here's how to stop this happening to you.

Get your main points down

Jot down each of the points you want to get across. You can do this on paper or quickly type the main points on your computer. For a very short note you'll be able to do it in your head.

You must sort out your ideas before you start writing or you run the risk of mixing in new ideas as you write.

Put your points in order

The next step is to arrange your points in order of importance. It may help to organise them into main points and subpoints, as in the example below.

Trade show arrangements ordered by importance

Set-up	Responsibility
	Date
	Delivery arrangements
Show	Dates
	Booth duty

Put your most important point first. When people are reading, they are most likely to remember the first thing they read. If your main point is a conclusion supported by points which follow, your readers can easily evaluate as they go.

You will nearly always put the most important point first. However, there are a couple of reasons why you would reverse the direction and put your main point last. One reason is when your readers literally won't know what you are talking about until you give them some background. Another reason is when the main point clashes with some preconceived idea of the reader and would lead to its immediate rejection.

Write your message

Turn each of your points into sentences and paragraphs, sticking to the point and saying it in as few words as possible. Include just one main idea per sentence and remember that sentences in a paragraph should relate.

When you are answering questions, deal with them one by one. Don't try and answer two questions with one sentence. Don't go back to a question once you have answered it.

Also be aware that people often skim over headings as they read. Each paragraph should stand by itself without the need to read the headings or the subject line. If it doesn't, reword the first sentence of the paragraph to include the information from the heading.

Revise and cut

Email messages should be preferably no more than two or three paragraphs. When you have written your message, you should reread your work. Revise and cut your message. Cut out wordiness. Check for ambiguity. Make sure you have used conversational language. Confirm that you have kept to one point at a time.

For a long message that cannot be shortened, consider sending it as an attachment and including just a summary in the email text. Alternatively, make the first paragraph a summary and then follow with the rest of the long message. Your readers are busy and they are not going to pore over a long story from you unless they are sure it is worthwhile. You need to convince them of this at the start.

WRITING REPLIES TO MESSAGES

When you are replying to a previous message or using information taken from earlier messages, there are some extra things to consider.

Don't change the subject when replying

Having a discussion by email is called a *conversation thread* or *thread*. As a general rule, you shouldn't change the subject of a message you are replying to because it helps people to keep track of the thread.

Mailers have sorting options which allow all messages with the same subject (ignoring the 'Re:' and 'Fwd:' component) to occur together in the selection list. This makes it easier to find all the mail relating to the thread. If you change the subject midway, you are thwarting this handy tool.

However, like a spoken conversation the subject can move as it goes on. You would then change the topic. To help you keep track, you may be able to keep the first part of the original subject, or indicate that the subject has changed. For example:

▓ **Original subject**

Subject: Spring catalogue schedule

Subject changed to:

Subject: Spring catalogue design
or
Subject: Catalogue design (formerly Spring catalogue schedule)

Include context

Decide how you are going to make sure your readers under-stand the context of your message. Your readers deal with many things and may have trouble recalling exactly what you are writing about if you forget to tell them. It's no fun getting an email message that simply says 'Yes' when you have sent other messages on the same subject.

It's easy for you to include a previous message with your reply. The reply or forward function usually opens a new message with the original message already included. You simply type your message at the front of it. If the reader needs to check the earlier correspondence, then it's there for them to read. If you are responding to several points or questions within the original message, you could insert your reply within the original message as in the example below.

■ Reply inserted into original message

> You are in charge of the trade show set-up next Monday.
> I have arranged for the equipment to be delivered to our
> stand (stand 8) at 8.30 a.m.
OK.
> The show runs from Tuesday to Friday. You are needed
> for booth duty at 8.30 a.m. each of these days.
I can't do Wednesday.

It is common to precede a quote from previous correspondence with >, as has been done in this example. This may happen automatically. You could also use different colours if you know that colours will appear on the recipient's screen.

Sometimes you are responding to only a part of the original message. In this case you may want to copy that part of the message and paste it into your message to make it clear what you are replying to.

The problem with these methods is that they may make the reader wade through too much context. It is often better for you to summarise the points. Two different ways of doing this are shown below. Choose the best method for ensuring that your readers can grasp the context quickly and so they know exactly what you are replying to.

▓ Responding with summarised points

> Set-up for trade show on Monday.
OK
> Booth duty Tuesday to Friday.
I can't do Wednesday.

Responding with summary in the text

Trade show is OK except for booth duty on Wednesday.

Respect the integrity of previous messages

While you may quote only a portion of a message or summarise it to reduce message length, you must not misrepresent the original message. And as with any other form of writing, you should acknowledge the source of the words, adhere to copyright restrictions, and seek permission to quote messages to a wider audience than was initially intended.

KEEPING YOUR READER IN MIND

Empathise with your readers by trying to imagine how they will receive your message. Try to predict their reaction. Will they be upset, confused or annoyed? Will they think that you have wasted their time?

Perhaps you can reshape the message to get a better reaction. You might also have to change the list of people receiving the message. (There is more about choosing who to send messages to in Chapter 3.)

Is the language or jargon over their head? Have you said things they might think are insensitive or distasteful? You need to be very aware of this when you're sending messages to people in other countries. Their English vocabulary could be small, and humour doesn't travel well.

Is your language inclusive and non-sexist? You may be surprised at the number of email messages which even today use 'Gentlemen' as the salutation, forgetting the females in the group.

Do you come across as someone who is courteous, friendly and enthusiastic, someone they want to listen to? Lively conversational language helps to create a good impression. Getting the right balance between formality and casualness conveys courtesy.

Have you spoken with confidence so that your readers feel they can accept your word as worthwhile? Uncertain writers include phrases like 'I hope you understand' and 'I hope you agree'. This does nothing for their message or career prospects.

Have you made negative statements? People don't like to be told no. Try to turn them into positive statements and give a reason when you have to say no. For example, 'I can't send it before Wednesday' could be written 'I will send it on Wednesday'.

Does it have a personal feel? You could say, 'We have mailed a cheque' or 'You will receive your cheque'. The second way is better because it's more personal.

EXPLAINING WHAT TO DO NEXT

Your message isn't complete if the readers don't know what to do after they have read it. A good email message is action-oriented. It makes it obvious what has to be done and who is to do it.

Tell them what to do

It's a mistake to think the action is self-evident. Your message should state what has to happen. If you don't want the readers to do anything, you can make this known by prefixing the message with 'For your information' or 'FYI'.

If you need the action to be completed by a certain time, again don't assume this is known. State it.

Make sure they know who

Make sure it says who is to take the action. When a message is sent to several people, it's often unclear who you want to do the work. Sometimes the readers may simply assume that you are taking the responsibility.

The reply in the earlier examples is not action-oriented. Someone has to organise a substitute for booth duty on Wednesday. Who? This can be fixed by inserting an action statement as shown below.

▓ This message is action-oriented

Trade show is OK except for booth duty on Wednesday. Please organise someone else for Wednesday.

MAKING SURE THE MESSAGE IS RIGHT

When you have finished writing your message, there are still a few things left to do before you can call it complete. In particular, you need to be sure that it's free of errors. Admittedly, many email messages are casual and you don't have to be fanatical about correctness in these. However, even some of these end up in the permanent record or being quoted, so some care is still needed.

Make sure you have put everything in

You want to save your readers and yourself time by getting things as complete as possible in this one message. You don't want them having to come back to you to ask questions that you could have answered if you had thought about it properly. Have you assumed the readers know something that they might not know? Have you covered all the issues that should be covered?

Check your facts

Your readers are going to depend and act on any facts that you give in your message. Are your facts correct? It isn't wise to rely on your memory alone. Check your facts.

Run a spelling check

Most mailers today have a spelling tool included. Become familiar with this tool so that you run it habitually before sending an email message.

If a spelling check can be activated via a key command or other shortcut, it's worthwhile remembering what this is so that you can quickly activate it when you have completed your message instead of having to find the menu item.

Unfortunately, spelling checkers don't pick up every mistake you may have made. For example, you may have typed 'though' when you meant 'thought'. You need to quickly reread your message, looking for mistakes like this.

Review the grammar and punctuation

Bad placement of a comma can sometimes change the meaning of a sentence. So while you are rereading, review your grammar and punctuation. Bad punctuation is usually best picked up by reading the message aloud. You might like to do this if you are not confident with punctuation.

Having covered all those things, your message is finished. Give it the one last test. Should you be sending this message as an email? Yes. Then hit the send button. You have completed a good email message.

THE MESSAGES NEED TO GO TO THE RIGHT PEOPLE

A beautifully laid out and clearly written email message is still no good until it reaches the right people, the people who can help you with your request.

The next chapter explains how to get your message out to the right people in the most effective way. You will learn about address books, mailing lists, shared folders and more.

KEY POINTS

- To compose email messages faster:
  - Keep your message short and find ways to reduce keystrokes.
  - Use templates and forms.
- When doing business by email:
  - Use a letterhead and the signature for company details.
  - Use an appropriate salutation and make it a personal communication.
- To get people to read your mail:
  - Write better messages and make them easy to reply to.
  - Use 'Urgent' when appropriate.

- — Get others to help you to understand the source of the problem.
- To write *concisely*:
  - — Start with a short and informative subject line.
  - — Use conversational language.
- To write *logically*:
  - — Jot down the main points and arrange by importance.
  - — Write the message using the outline and then revise and cut.
- To *empathise* with the reader:
  - — Try to see it through the readers' eyes and predict their reactions.
- To make a message *action-oriented*:
  - — State what has to be done next, by whom and by when.
- To get the message *right:*
  - — Check that everything that is needed is included and correct.

EXERCISES

With these exercises you will learn to apply clear writing techniques to your own email messages.

1. **Select the longest business-related email message you have sent recently.**

   Evaluate it on a scale of 1 to 5 for each of the characteristics listed below. Selecting 1 indicates that it doesn't have the characteristic, while 5 indicates that it uses the characteristic very well.

	Doesn't have			Uses very well	
Has a short, informative subject	1	2	3	4	5
Uses simple words and short sentences	1	2	3	4	5
Uses lively active speech	1	2	3	4	5
Is logical, with the important points first	1	2	3	4	5
Includes context	1	2	3	4	5
The tone is suited to the reader	1	2	3	4	5
Has an action specified	1	2	3	4	5
Has all the information needed	1	2	3	4	5
Is error-free	1	2	3	4	5

2. **Rewrite the message trying to improve the weakest areas.**

3. **Read your rewritten message aloud.**
   Does it flow smoothly? Are there any words that you wouldn't use in conversation?

chapter 3

Who should I send email messages to?

Email has made it almost too easy to send messages to a lot of people. There are harried workers in offices everywhere wasting time sifting through and reading all the clutter that is sent. You won't want to add to the woes of your overworked colleagues. So ask yourself before you send something, 'Who really needs this message? Should I copy everyone on this reply?'

This chapter will help you to get the answers to these questions right. To begin, it is useful to have an address book which has the right addresses. The address book can also be used to create mail groups for distributing information to groups of people.

USING YOUR ADDRESS BOOK

Email addresses can be cumbersome and accuracy is essential. You will want to reduce the number of times you have to type them. Your address book is the tool to use so you don't have to remember them. There are two types of address books—company address books and personal address books.

The company address book contains the name and email address of every person in the company who uses email. It is particularly useful when there are several people with the same name. A slight variation, such as using their middle initial, has to be used to differentiate people with the same name. Without the address book, you won't know this variation. The company address book is set up and maintained by the email administrator.

Most mailers also include a personal address book facility where you can keep your personal addresses. This may be integrated into the company address book facility. Even so, the addresses in your personal address book are for your own use and no one else has access to them.

Putting addresses in your personal address book

A personal address book entry allows you to type the person's name, the email address and a nickname or alias. (Later in the chapter there is an explanation of where you can get addresses from and what correct addresses look like.) You may also be able to include other information, such as street addresses and telephone and fax numbers. The example in Figure 3.1 has tabs at the top for adding this type of information.

If a person's address or other details change after you have created an entry, you simply display their entry and replace the old information with the new information.

The most accurate way to put an address into your personal address book is when you receive an email message from the person. You copy the return email address and paste it into a new address book entry. Some mailers make it even easier, by allowing you to point to an email address and then select the 'Add to address book' function. The address book will appear with a new entry and the basic information already added. You just have to add the extra details. Others will, if

Figure 3.1 An address book entry

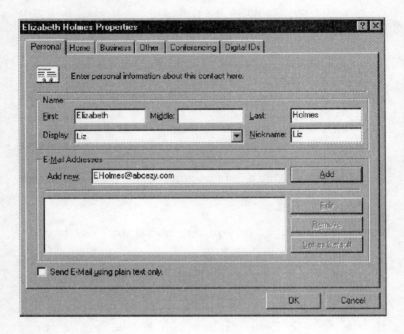

you wish, automatically put the addresses of everyone you reply to in your address book.

Be diligent in putting entries in your address book. Without this, you will be constantly looking up business cards or searching old email messages to find addresses.

I work with a lot of people from other countries. I can never remember how to spell their names, so it's quicker to use their initials as nicknames.

—Lou, Executive Assistant

You can use any nickname you like when you are creating an entry, because the person's full email address will be inserted into the message you send. However, be aware that some mailers insert the nickname as a comment with the address, and it may be displayed in the message received by the recipient. So don't use a nickname which may offend the recipient.

Using your personal address book

There is a lot of variation in the way address books are displayed and used, so you will need to check your instruction manual or on-screen help facility to understand how your mailer works. Some will automatically look up the address book when you begin typing a name in the recipient list. You only have to type the beginning of the name and the mailer completes the rest of it from its address book. Others will display the address book if you click on a recipient field and allow you to choose from the entries in your address book. Others require you to select the 'Address book' option from the menu bar.

It will pay you to learn the quickest way of using the address. If you think you might not be doing this with the best method, put a priority on finding out how.

Here's a potential problem you may encounter when you are using a corporate email system. You may be able to specify which address book to use when a name is in both your personal address book and the company address book. Be aware that if you select your personal address book, then you must keep it up to date with any address changes that occur in the company address book.

USING PERSONAL MAIL GROUPS

Members of teams need to send mail to the same group of people again and again. Even with an address book, it's very inefficient to type the list of team members each time you send a message. The answer to this problem is a mail group.

A *mail group* (also called a *mailing list* or *distribution list*) is an address book entry which has the addresses of two or more people.

Creating a personal mail group

You can create a mail group and give the group a name using the 'Mail group' function of your address book. There is probably a facility which allows you to type the addresses of the people in the group or to select the names from the address book, as in Figure 3.2.

You can select as many names as you want and make as many different groups as you want. The names on the email messages you send will be in the order they are listed in your mail group, so it's best to select the names alphabetically when you create your group entry.

Sending to a personal mail group

To send a message to the people in the group you don't have to type all of their names, just the name of the group in the recipient list, as in Figure 3.3. You can send a message to more than one group at a time by typing the names of all the groups you want to send to.

When you send the message, the mailer substitutes the names of the members of the group instead of your group name. The people who receive the message usually see all of the names as if you typed them individually, not the name of the group.

Considerations for using personal mail groups

Because the names of the people in the list are not usually displayed when you are composing the message, you may forget who is in the group. You don't want to send mail

Figure 3.2 Creating a mail group

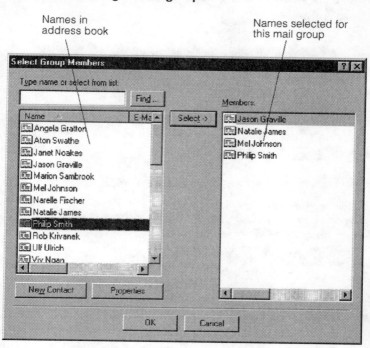

Names in address book

Names selected for this mail group

indiscriminately, so you need to put careful thought into who comprises your groups.

When there is an overlap of people in the groups, some mailers will remove the duplicate names and only send the message once, while others which don't remove duplicates will send multiple copies of the message. You should find out whether your mailer removes duplicates as this may influence the way you set up your groups.

You also need to keep your groups up to date. When people leave the company or change jobs, remember to alter your personal mail groups accordingly. When a person's email address changes, you usually only have to change the individual

Figure 3.3 Addressing a group

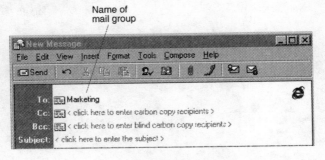

Name of
mail group

I had some 'marginal' members in
my distribution list. Only about
half of my messages were relevant to
these people. One of them com-
plained, so I broke my big
distribution list into smaller lists to
target people better. Unfortunately,
there was an overlap in the small
lists, so some people then received
two copies when I addressed a
couple of groups at the same time. I
then had to fix that.

—Ali, Product Manager

address book entry and your
mail groups will pick up the
right address from there.

USING COMPANY-WIDE MAIL GROUPS

On corporate email systems,
company-wide mail groups
may also be available to you.
A company-wide mail group
is similar to a personal mail
group, except the list of mem-
bers in the group is created and maintained by the email
administrator.

Company-wide mail groups are used for grouping peers
and other working teams. They are particularly useful for
raising questions or sharing information with your colleagues.
They are also a good forum for canvassing opinions and
collecting ideas.

The names of the company-wide mail groups will usually
appear in your company address book. Typically the names
will have an identifying character, such as '$', in front of them

or be in a separate subsection of the address book. For example, there may be groups called $allstaff, $manufacturing, $sales, $admin and $finance.

Sending to a company-wide mail group

You use a company-wide mail group in the same way as a personal mail group. You type the name of the group you want to send to in the recipient field and the message is sent to every one in the group. However, with company-wide mail groups the name of the group is usually displayed, rather than the names of the individuals. This is fortunate, because company-wide mail groups can often be very large.

Considerations for using company-wide mail groups

Before you use a company-wide mail group find out who is on the list. '$admin' may represent a certain group of people to you, when it's actually a totally different team. There is often no way for you to display this information, so you will have to ask. Asking in advance could save you the embarrassment of sending a message to an inappropriate group.

Always use company-wide mail groups with some discretion. Remember that your message is being sent to a wide group of people. You don't want to bother them all with a question that could have been answered readily by asking just one or two people.

Some companies restrict the use of mail groups because the privilege is abused by people sending frivolous or unnecessary messages to a large group of people. Understand your company's policy for using the group before sending a message to it. Also watch for any conventions used by the group for posting messages.

When a message is sent to a large group of people seeking their help or opinion, quite a lot of people may respond (often

> *People started using the 'companyall' mail group to sell their cars and such. These messages go to everybody including the highest executives.*
>
> —Rick, Email Administrator
>
> ---
>
> *We put 'Q' for question, 'H' for help, 'A' for answer and 'I' for info at the start of the subject. This helps the recipients to decide whether to read it.*
>
> —Chloe, Systems Engineer
>
> ---
>
> *I am on a general distribution list. Someone complained to the list about getting five copies of every message. People replied to the whole list, giving explanations and opinions. I ended up with 30 of these time-wasting messages. I figure that person got 150 of them.*
>
> —Linda, Secretary

with duplicate suggestions). This can generate extra mail for everyone in the group. Rather than everyone receiving the replies, ask for people to reply only to you. You can gather the responses, consolidate them and then distribute a summary to the whole group.

When you are replying to questions, consider whether the answer is of relevance to everyone or whether you are better off replying just to the person who asked the question. This can save a lot of unnecessary email traffic.

If you are getting multiple copies of messages, it could be because you are listed in several mail groups and the mailer isn't removing duplicate names. You can treat this as one of the hazards of being multitalented, or ask the email administrator to remove you from the lists that are irrelevant to you.

Joining a company-wide mail group

Companies will often automatically add you to the groups that are relevant to your job or profession. However, if you are not part of a list that you would like to belong to, ask your email administrator to add you to the group.

If you would like to be able to reach a group of peers

and a company-wide mail group has not been set up, then your email administrator should be able to set one up. Alternatively, you could use a personal mail group. The advantage of a company-wide group is that all group members have access to the distribution list without each having to establish and maintain their own personal mail groups. Also, with large international groups you are unlikely to know everyone who should be in the group and it's difficult to keep up with the changes. It's easier for these to be centrally managed as a company-wide group.

USING SHARED FOLDERS

On some corporate email systems, shared folders can be used instead of company-wide mail groups. Shared folders are also known by other names, such as *conferences*, *bulletin boards* and *noticeboards*.

A *shared folder* is a folder where email messages are stored and can be accessed by a group of people. A shared folder is just like one of your personal folders, except that the messages in the folder can be viewed by all of the people given access to the folder, not just you. Shared folders are created by your email administrator.

It is usually possible to restrict access to a shared folder so that only those who need to receive the information can read it. Access is granted by the email administrator.

Reading a shared folder

Shared folders may be displayed together with your personal folders, or they may be displayed in a place used especially for shared folders. You view the messages in a shared folder in the same way as you view the messages in your own personal folders.

When a new message is received into the shared folder it

will be flagged in the same way as unread messages in your inbox. This way you know a message is there to be read.

Sending to a shared folder

Shared folders are an alternative to mail groups for sharing information. The difference is that sending a message to a shared folder sends just one email message to the folder, whereas sending to a mail group posts an email message to every person on the list. Also, people can browse the contents of a shared folder when they are ready, rather than getting an email message in their inbox which they then have to process.

The method for putting a message in a shared folder varies. Often this is done by sending a message to the folder name, in much the same way as you would send a message to a company-wide mail group. Some shared folders are managed by an administrator. In this case you send what you want to put into the folder to the administrator who then puts it into the folder for you.

Some uses for shared folders

We set up a shared folder for general interest notices—advertisements for group theatre tickets, birth announcements, 'for sale' notices and such. People only need to look at these if they are interested.

—Rick, Email Administrator

Shared folders can be helpful for conserving disk space on the corporate email system because there is only one copy of the message instead of a copy sent to everyone in the group.

Shared folders also have the advantage of keeping a history of email messages in one place. When new members join the team, they can review the history simply by browsing the contents of the folder. Without this, copies of old messages would have to be sent to the new team member.

WHO TO SEND MESSAGES TO

The recipient list is where you put the addresses of the people you want to send messages to. Figure 3.4 shows the three types of recipients available on most mailers. You can put more than one address in any of these lists.

To. The people in the 'To:' list are those who are the primary recipients of the message. They are expected to action the message.

Cc. The people in the 'Cc:' list are 'carbon copied' or 'courtesy copied' on the message. They are not expected to action the message but can reply if they want to.

Bcc. The people in the 'Bcc:' list are 'blind copied' on the message. The message is provided to them for their information only. The 'Bcc:' list is never displayed, so other recipients are totally unaware that the message has been blind copied.

Use 'To:' for action

The people you include on the 'To:' list should have a direct interest in the content of the message. These are the people who the message is really for. You want them to read it carefully and to take any action you are requesting.

You should ensure that the people on the 'To:' list are the right people. Do these people have the authority and knowledge to act on your request? Do you want everyone on this list to act in some way, or just one of them? Maybe some should be moved to the 'Cc:' list instead.

Figure 3.4 The recipient elements of an email message

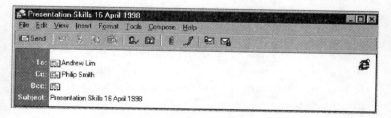

Check your message to confirm that everyone on your 'To:' list will find it relevant. Ensure that it has been written with each of them in mind. When there is more than one recipient, make sure the action you want each to take is clear.

Readers can sometimes put an unwanted interpretation on the way your list is ordered. Avoid this by listing the recipients in alphabetical order unless one person is clearly of much higher rank, in which case you would put that person first.

Use 'Cc:' for information

The 'Cc:' list is for the other people who would have an interest in the message. You are supplying it to them for their information, not for their action.

This is the list which is most abused. Since the introduction of email, people seem to want to copy everyone who may have a passing interest in a subject. As with the 'To:' list, consider the relevance of this message to the people you have copied.

> *I think too many people send copies of their messages just to protect themselves and to grandstand their activities.*
>
> —*Robin, Clerical Assistant*

You need to understand the politics of your office situation, but remember that copying people can backfire if your motives are transparent or your mail is perceived to be a nuisance.

You should be quite ruthless in cutting your 'Cc:' list. Only copy people who will get some genuine benefit from reading the information you have sent. It's best for the 'Cc:' list also to be in alphabetical order.

Use 'Bcc:' with caution

Blind copies can give the undesirable implication that you are going behind a person's back. You should think very carefully before using this feature. There will be few cases where it is really necessary.

People sometimes use 'Bcc:' to suppress the full list of names in a personal mail group when there are a lot of people in the group. Even though you only type a single name for the whole group, when your message is sent the names of the individual members are substituted. For a large group there will be a long list of names. Some mailers display the list of recipients with only one name per line, which means the recipients have to skip over pages of names before they get to the actual message.

When the group name is put in the 'Bcc:' field, the recipients receive a message with their name in the 'To:' list and no other names. The only disadvantage of this approach is that the recipients don't know that the message has been sent to a group rather than to themselves individually.

WHO TO REPLY AND FORWARD TO

Replying will open a new message addressed to the sender or all recipients of the original message. The original message is often included for you to use as context. Sometimes you have to select the 'Forward' option or 'Reply with history' option to open it with the original email message included.

Forwarding opens a new message with the original message included. The recipient list is empty, ready for you to choose who it is to be sent to. The idea is for you to send the whole message on for someone else to handle or use. You can pass it on with or without your own comments. (There are also automatic forwarding and reply options, which are explained in Chapter 8.)

Know the difference between types of replies

You usually have the choice of 'Reply to sender' which replies just to the sender of the original message, or 'Reply to all' which replies to all recipients of the original message.

> *A notice from the personnel manager went out to all staff. I took exception to a small point and wanted to quietly raise my objection. I forgot to reply just to the sender and it was blasted to everybody in the company. I was presented with the 'Email Novice of the Year' award at our annual sales meeting.*
>
> *—Ann, Sales Manager*

'Reply to all' is a regular source of email embarrassment. Make sure you know the difference between 'Reply to sender' and 'Reply to all' and know how to make your mailer use the one you want. If there is only one reply button, there will usually be a method of tailoring this to either 'Reply to sender' or 'Reply to all' as its normal way of working. Set this to 'Reply to sender' so that you'll have to make a special choice to 'Reply to all'.

Choose the recipients

Before you send the message, look at the 'To:' and 'Cc:' list the original sender used and assess whether your reply will be relevant to everyone on this list. If your reply will be relevant to just some people, you could 'Reply to all' and then go through the list and remove names. Alternatively, you could 'Reply to sender' and add a few extra names.

In the interests of reducing the email burden, your first choice should be to reply to the sender only. Include others in the reply only if they will get genuine benefit from your response. Even though the originator has copied a huge list of people, it doesn't mean you have to continue the nuisance.

REORGANISING THE ORGANISATION WITH EMAIL

Just because it's easy to copy the boss, do you need to? Indiscriminate copying up the hierarchy is causing disruption in some organisations. Organisations which have an orderly hierarchical structure are the most affected by this new office phenomenon.

Information flows more freely

In the past a manager may have seen little of the work in progress. Now it is written in email messages instead of being in random conversations. Managers are often copied by at least some members of the team. Keeping the boss informed can become a political competition. It's an old game, but be aware that the rules have changed somewhat because of the ease of passing on information.

Actually, being more in touch is not a bad thing. Many organisations are finding that email is helping teams to work together more effectively and to be more responsive.

Respect the established hierarchy

It can cause problems when everyone wants to go to the 'top' rather than using the established hierarchy which was designed to streamline information handling.

> *I was getting dozens of email messages from field engineers every day. I ended up having to say I would only reply to mail from regional managers.*
>
> *—Alfonso, Head Engineer*

Some organisations have found they need to introduce rules to reinstate the traditional processes. Another way is for people to send the message back with a polite standard note reinforcing the proper procedure. Failure to implement a sensible method can lead to some people in the organisation having an intolerable workload.

Don't go over people's heads

Another feature of email is that many executives handle their mail directly without screening by personal assistants.

> *I'm amazed at what some people send through. They seem to forget I'm really here at the other end.*
>
> —*Margaret, Business Executive*

Knowing this, some staff take it as an opportunity to go straight to the 'very top'. Resist this temptation.

A senior manager will usually pass your message to the right person to handle first before allowing it to escalate. By going over people's heads, you will have achieved little and run the risk of annoying important people. Prevent false bravado and impoliteness by always remembering the person, anticipating how they will react, being sensitive to their workload and considering others in the chain of command.

This isn't to say you won't use email to reach someone who you would otherwise be unable to contact. Rather, you need to consider the consequences before you do.

Harness the power without abusing it

The general effect of email is to flatten hierarchical organisations, which can be a very painful process in some companies. While this may make your organisation more egalitarian, it's unlikely to make it less political. Your best defence is to be aware that it happens, so that you are neither outsmarted by nor unwittingly hurtful to others.

You want to harness the power of email to get information on the move effectively without causing undue stress and workload. The best way you can do this is by consciously choosing precisely who is to receive your messages.

GETTING ADDRESSES

To send an email message to a particular person, you need their email address. The address you use will vary according to whether you are addressing a person within your company who uses your corporate email system or a person outside your company who uses the Internet. People from outside your company will also want to know your address so that they can send email messages to you.

Addresses for people within your company

When you are using a corporate email system, to address people within your company, you can usually type their name only, such as 'Narelle Fischer', 'Narelle_Fischer', 'Fischer Narelle', 'Fischer.N' or some other variation. Some companies use account numbers rather than names, in which case the address could be something like 'V703139'. The easiest way is to select the address from the company address book.

Addresses for people on the Internet

You can send email messages to people in other companies when your email system is connected to the Internet. To address people on the Internet, you need to know their Internet address. You usually get this in the same way as you get a person's street address—from their business card or letterhead, by word of mouth and such like. There is no email equivalent to a telephone directory which has every Internet email address. The best way is to ask the person directly, write them a letter or send a fax.

There are directory services on the Internet which have some email addresses. You can access these directories with your Web browser, or there may be a feature which gives you easy access to them from within your mailer. When you need the address of someone you don't otherwise know how to contact, you might like to try these directories.

It is essential that you get every part of an Internet email address right. This includes typing upper and lower case letters exactly as written. Just as with paper mail addresses, getting one thing wrong can mean your mail is delivered to the wrong place or returned to you undelivered. The next section,

'Understanding Internet addresses', shows you what a correct Internet address looks like.

With some corporate email systems, you need to indicate that the address you have typed is an Internet address rather than an internal address. This will require you to put some special indicator like 'Internet' at the end of the address. Ask if this is the case with your system.

Addresses from mail you receive

The easiest way to get the correct address is to receive a message from the person. When you reply, their address is automatically put in the message.

The return address will occasionally be wrong when the original address has been translated to go across the Internet. Also, some mailers lose the end of long addresses. When people experience this problem with their mail they usually put their correct Internet address in the body of their email message.

Modern mailers recognise an Internet address within a message and underline it. If yours does this, you'll probably be able to create a message to this address simply by clicking on the underlined address. A new message will be opened with the address already inserted.

Giving out your Internet email address

You may want to give your Internet email address to people so that they can send messages to you. You may also want to put it on your business card or include it in your signature. The email address to use is usually the same as the one that appears on messages you send.

However, if you are using a corporate email system, ask your email administrator what is the right way to write your email address as an Internet email address. You may need more than your internal address and sometimes there can be a friendlier version than appears on your email messages.

UNDERSTANDING INTERNET ADDRESSES

An Internet address has two parts: who the message is to; and what computer they are on. The first and second parts are separated by an @ sign. For example:

▓ **Sample Internet email address**

n_fischer@aaaint.com.au
The person is 'N. Fischer'
The computer is 'aaaint.com.au'

You may notice that email from the Internet sometimes has more information in the email address, like the examples below. These extra bits are comments typically giving the sender's name. This is helpful where the sender's name is not clear from the address itself. When a message is received, some mailers display the name from the comment, rather than the email address. The mailer ignores these comments when it is sending the message. It doesn't matter whether they are included or not when you are replying. However, when the message is sent, some mailers insert the name or nickname you have used in your address book as a comment.

▓ **An Internet email address with comments**

Narelle Fischer   <n_fischer@aaaint.com.au> or
n_fischer@aaaint.com.au (Narelle Fischer)

The first part has the person's name

You will find there is a lot of variation in the format of the first part of the address. This is the part which says which person it is for. Some addresses may use just initials or first names, others use two names separated with underscore characters or periods, some may have upper and lower case letters, others may have only lower case letters. There is no way of knowing what is right other than typing it exactly as it was given to you.

The second part has the domain address

The second part of the address is more uniform. This is the part which says which computer it is to go to. This is known as the *domain address*. The domain address will have two or more parts separated by periods and will be all in lower case.

The last part of the domain address says the type of organisation that is being addressed or which country the computer is in. Some addresses have both an organisation type and a country code. The current organisation types and some country codes are given below. Because the number of Internet users is increasing rapidly, new organisation types are being introduced these are also given below.

▓ Internet organisation type codes

com	commercial
edu	educational
org	non-profit organisation
net	networking organisation
gov	government installation
mil	military organisation

New Internet organisation type codes

nom	personal web pages
firm	company or firm
arts	arts and cultural sites
rec	recreation and entertainment sites
store	businesses selling goods

info	information services
web	web-related entity

Some Internet country codes

au	Australia
jp	Japan
se	Sweden
th	Thailand
uk	United Kingdom
us	United States

The domain address may not always specify the actual country where the person is working. With international companies you may address the mail to a central computer in Canada, for example, and this forwards the mail to their branch computer in Korea.

The rest of the address gives the name of the company, organisation, university and such like. It is also used to identify which computer within the company when there is more than one. The example below shows how to interpret an Internet address. You will find it quite easy to do the same with addresses you use.

▨ Interpreting an Internet email address

n_fischer@aaaint.com.au
is addressing the person 'N. Fischer' at the company 'aaaint' which is a 'commercial' site in 'Australia'.

When the person you are addressing is a small business user or a personal user, then the company name is likely to be the name of their Internet service provider rather than their own company.

HANDLING UNDELIVERED AND MISADDRESSED MAIL

If you don't get the recipient's address right or the computer at the receiving end isn't working, your message won't be delivered and a notification will usually be sent to you. Read the body of any notification messages telling you that mail has been undelivered because it may only be delayed.

Mail can be delayed

Your message will mostly be delivered within minutes. When the mail network is experiencing unusual delays it will send a notice warning you of this delay.

This doesn't mean your message won't be delivered. Perhaps the computer at the other end is temporarily unavailable. Don't resend your message, because further attempts will be made to deliver your original message.

Mail can be undelivered

When a message can't be delivered, it is returned to you with a notice. The notice will give you the reason why the message didn't get through but it may be very technical.

The most likely cause is that you made a mistake in the address. If the notice says this, then correct the address and try again. It could be due to problems with the destination computer or within the network. In this case, try sending the message again.

You can usually assume that your message has been safely delivered unless you receive a notice telling you otherwise. However, mail can occasionally go astray without reporting to you, so if you are kept waiting for a very long time for a reply, follow-up with another email message or telephone call.

You can get misaddressed mail

You may receive mail that wasn't meant for you because the sender has typed the wrong address. It's polite to return the message to the sender, telling them you received it in error. This will save you getting more mail from this unwanted source.

INCOMING MAIL IS NEXT

From this chapter and the previous chapter you know how to write effective messages quickly and how to get them to reach the right audience. This has equipped you to handle your outgoing mail quickly.

The next chapter helps you with your incoming mail. You will learn time-saving techniques for handling the messages that you receive in your inbox.

KEY POINTS

- To get the addresses right:
  - Use the company address book for internal addresses.
  - Type Internet addresses exactly as supplied.
  - Keep names and addresses in your personal address book.
- Mail groups are used to send mail to groups of people.
  - Set up personal mail groups to save having to type a list of names.
  - Remember to tailor and review your personal mail groups.
  - Follow the established rules and conventions when posting mail to a company-wide mail group.

- Shared folders are another way of sharing information.
- When you are sending email messages:
  - Use 'To:' for recipient action.
  - Use 'Cc:' for recipient information.
  - Use 'Bcc:' for blind copies with caution.
- When you are replying to email messages:
  - Use 'Reply to sender' as your normal choice.
  - Be selective about who you include in your reply.
- Email is changing the way organisations work.
  - Be aware of this and its implications for the way you need to work.
  - Always remember there is a person at the other end, so don't be brash.

EXERCISES

In these exercises you will review your current work habits to see if you can improve the ways you send email messages.

1. **Look at a sample of email messages you have sent and received. Do you think the recipient list should be changed?**

2. **Have you set up some personal mail groups?**
   Review each of these groups and confirm that they include the right people. Reorder the groups and create new groups if necessary.

3. **Do you think email is changing the way your organisation works? What implications does this have for the way you use email?**

chapter 4

Email is taking over my life—what should I do?

Is email getting you down? Has it become the top priority of your day? Do you never feel on top it? Email has become so compelling in its demand to be answered that it is overwhelming for many people.

There is help. You have the power to regain balance in your working life. All it takes is a little organisation and putting email back in its place as a tool to help you, not to control you.

For those for whom email hasn't reached these burdensome heights, be warned: it can happen almost without your noticing. You can avoid overload by using time-saving habits early.

You'll find techniques in this chapter to help you organise your email messages and some tips to help you organise your time better.

HANDLING YOUR EMAIL MESSAGES MORE QUICKLY

A common trap for the unwary email user is giving every message the same amount of attention. What you should be doing is deciding the importance of each message and responding accordingly. (The section 'Managing your time' at the end of this chapter gives some guidance on how to decide what is important for you to be doing each day.)

Process each message only once

Resolve to handle each message only once. As soon as you read it, act on it according to its importance. Decide to do one of four things:

- Delete it.
- Save it for reading or action at an appropriate time.
- Pass it on.
- Act on it.

Scan each message. Read the subject. Read the first paragraph. If necessary, read the first lines of key paragraphs. This should give you enough information to decide. Now decide.

Form a habit of making this type of quick decision each time you read an email message. It will save you a lot of time. Leaving messages lying in your inbox with no evaluation causes you to read them again and again. This is the same as shuffling paper around and is a total waste of time.

Delete it

Irrelevant email messages are often called *junk email*. Receiving junk email messages is a fact of life. Give these messages the treatment they deserve and don't waste your time worrying about them. Delete them without a second thought and don't feel guilty.

Typically this mail will be announcement notices, mail from mail groups and unwanted unsolicited mail. (There is more on this later in the chapter.) You will be able to recognise most of it immediately from the sender's address or the subject.

Some of the information you get from mail groups will be of interest and some won't. Judge this by the subject and delete irrelevant messages without further ado.

If you are finding that you are getting an overwhelming amount of junk email from a particular source, then it's worth taking some action to eliminate it. If it's from an individual, ask them to stop copying you on the unwanted information. Ask to be removed from the company-wide mail groups that are only sending you irrelevant mail. If you think people are using company-wide mail groups to send messages that are irrelevant to most people, ask for policy guidelines to be established on the use of these groups.

Save it

Messages that you save fall into two categories:

- reading material; and
- those you set aside because they are of lower priority or it isn't the right time to work on them yet.

When you set a message aside, file it where you can find it later. An 'Action pending' file is a good place. Don't leave it in your inbox to be shuffled around. Some mailers delete messages which have been read and not filed. If yours is like this, then you must file any message you want to read again later.

Question the value of all reading material. If it is serving no useful purpose, delete it and consider cutting yourself off from its source, such as getting off the mailing list.

Pass it on

Thinking you can do all the work yourself is one of the top causes of overload. If you aren't the right person to handle the task, pass it on. It takes very little time to forward an email message with a quick note—perhaps as little as For Your

> *I scan reading material. If it looks useful I print it so that I can read it while I'm travelling or waiting for an appointment.*
>
> —*Janet, Sales Manager*

Action (or FYA), and it's gone. Copy the sender if you think they need to know who their new contact is.

Act on it

If you can handle the message with a quick response straight away, do it now to get rid of it. The emphasis here is on *quick*. If it's going to take more than a few moments' thought or a short paragraph to answer, then it should be handled in line with the tasks and priorities planned for your day.

Alternatively, you may choose to process all of the mail, clear the items you can handle quickly and then leave the longer items to process throughout the day. If you do this, don't let routine mail run overtime.

> *I do my mail in two sessions, the first to get the high-priority items and a later session to clear the rest.*
>
> —*Brendan, Account Manager*

SETTING UP YOUR FILING SYSTEM

A good filing system is the key to being able to handle each message only once. Each message will have a logical place to go. You will be able to put it there quickly and find it again easily when you need it.

Review your current filing scheme

You probably have some folders already created and have been filing messages in them. Review your current filing scheme and consider any problems it's giving you.

- Do you have difficulty deciding which folder to put a message in?
- Do you have trouble deciding which folder a message is likely to be in when you want to find it later?
- Do you have some folders which are bulging with assorted mixed messages that should be broken into subcategories (folders within folders)?
- Do you have some folders which have almost no messages and could be removed?
- Are your subcategories logical and easy to find?
- Can you identify the messages which still have action outstanding from those which are complete?
- Is your inbox full of messages that have been read and not filed? Is your filing scheme (or lack of it) influencing this?
- Are there any other things you like or dislike about your current filing scheme?

Now you are ready either to revamp your current scheme or to start afresh with a more manageable arrangement.

Choose a new filing scheme

There are four basic schemes used for filing. Think about the messages you handle and choose a scheme that suits you:

- alphabetic
- numeric
- subject
- geographic.

Subject-based schemes are the most popular with email users. Assuming you have chosen a subject-based scheme, now you need to decide which subject categories suit your work. If you can create subfolders within folders, start with broad categories and make subcategories where necessary. In addition

Figure 4.1 A filing scheme

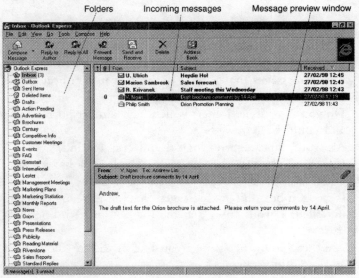

to your subject folders you may also want others for 'Action pending', 'Awaiting reply', 'Drafts' and such like.

Before you settle on your final scheme, consider the practicalities of your mailer. Are the folders displayed on the screen? Where? How many can you see at a glance? Look at the example in Figure 4.1. This scheme has a large number of folders and is probably not very efficient because of the need to search up and down the list.

When you have more folders than can be displayed on the screen at the one time, you can reorganise them for more efficient processing. Folders are usually displayed alphabetically so active and inactive folders are mixed together. Get the active folders to the top of the list by starting the name with 'AA' or making them subfolders of a folder called 'Active'. Then you will only have to scroll down the list occasionally instead of all the time.

Figure 4.2 An improved filing scheme

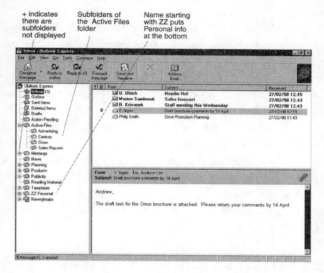

When the subject is no longer as busy, you can rename it or move it out of the 'Active' folder. This is generally quite easy to do. Make sure it's easy to do on your mailer before you settle for this arrangement.

The example in Figure 4.2 shows the previous scheme reorganised to be more efficient. Many of the folders have been made subcategories and a folder for active items has been created. The folder list is now shorter and more manageable, and most incoming mail could now be dropped into the appropriate file without changing the folder display. When one of the subfolders is needed, it can be easily displayed by clicking on the main category icon.

Set up the folders

You now have all you need to finalise your filing scheme. If you radically change your filing scheme it's going to take you a while to change things. Why not set aside a couple of hours to get the job done? It will pay off with time savings almost immediately.

If you can, rename your existing folders so they don't get mixed up with the new ones you are creating. Start the names with 'ZZ' so they are out of your way at the bottom of the folder list.

Set up your new filing scheme by creating each of the new folders. Then, go through your old messages folder by folder and move them into the appropriate new folders. Delete each old folder as it is emptied.

Take this opportunity to do a good clean-up as well, rather than just moving the messages. Delete the old ones you don't need. Be ruthless and delete as many as possible. (If you're having trouble deciding what you should or shouldn't delete, read Chapter 5.)

AUTOMATING FILING WITH FILTERS

With some mailers it's possible to let them make some of the routine filing decisions. While a growing number are offering this capability, there is great variation in what they can do and their ease of use. This section explains the types of things they can do, so you can find out what your mailer is capable of.

Understand filters

The mailer can search a message looking for clues about its origin, its subject and other criteria, and act in accordance with what it finds. This is called message *filtering*. (Filters are also known as *rules* or *agents*.)

Some mailers work only on incoming email messages, while others work on outgoing messages as well. The types of things you can do with message filtering are:

• Automatically file messages from a mailing list into an appropriate folder so that clutter is removed from your inbox.

- Delete unwanted messages.
- Respond to customer messages with a polite standard response so that they know action is under way.
- Respond to specific text in the subject or body of the message, like 'Send sales statistics'.
- Detect messages from the boss and make a special alert sound or raise their priority so that they sit at the top of your list.

Your mailer may let you do only one action per message, like file it in a folder or delete it. Other mailers allow you to do multiple actions, like doing all of these to the one message—send an automatic response, file it, change the subject and forward it to another person for action.

Your mailer may allow only simple choices—for example, if the subject contains the words 'press release', then file the message in the 'News' folder. Others allow more complex decisions—for example, if the subject contains the words 'press release' and the sender is 'PR agency' or 'marketing department', then file the message in the 'Press release drafts' folder, but file in the 'News' folder if the sender is any other source.

Set up your filters

Even the most basic filtering capability is a benefit. It can help you with routine filing and deleting, thereby reducing the number of messages you have to handle individually. If you have a lot of email that you routinely file, it's worth the effort to find out how to use filtering for these simple tasks.

In the mailer illustrated in Figure 4.3, you can see that setting a simple filter to file email messages is very easy.

Your mailer may have a more complex scripting language. Even so, because you are going to start with just some simple filing activities, the process shouldn't be too difficult to learn. If you are having trouble setting up your first filter, see if your

Figure 4.3 Setting a filter

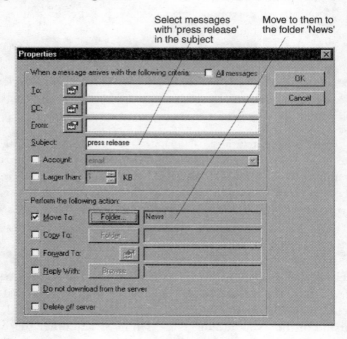

email administrator or software help desk can guide you. Extra filters should involve just a few small changes from there.

Organise your filters logically

When you are using more than one filter, you have to consider the order in which the filters are applied. For example, you may want to apply the following two filters to your incoming messages:

▓ Multiple filtering criteria

1. If the subject contains the words 'press release', then file the message in the folder 'News'.

2.   If the sender contains the word 'parliament', then file the
      message in the folder 'Government'.

Using these criteria, what happens if the parliamentary
office sends a press release? The message would match both
criteria, so which folder would the message be put in? Your
mailer may work in the following way. A message is compared
against each of the criteria until it finds a match. The filtering
process for that message then stops and the rest of the filtering
criteria are ignored. In that case, if the filters are in their
current order, the message would match the first criteria and
be filed in the folder 'News'. It would not reach the second
choice. If the criteria were the other way round, the message
would be put in the folder 'Government'.

So you can see that the order of the filtering criteria
matters for any message that meets two or more criteria. You
need to get the order of the filtering criteria right for what
you want to happen. If your messages only ever match one
filtering criteria, the order of the filters doesn't matter.

Other mailers may handle messages which match two criteria
differently. You may need to experiment a little with some
messages that meet multiple criteria to find out what happens.

Filtering can require you to think a bit like a computer
programmer. This is even more so for more complex filtering.
However, the requirements for simple filtering should be easy
enough for you to master. After you have the basic filing tasks
set up, you can decide if you have the skill or interest to do more.

HANDLING UNWANTED UNSOLICITED EMAIL

If you use the Internet, and particularly if you have joined
Internet mailing lists, it won't be long before you know about
spam. *Spam* is unwanted unsolicited email. The name is said
to come from a *Monty Python* sketch where the canned
luncheon meat 'Spam' is served with every meal. Internet

spam can be like that, repetitive and distasteful. You need to know what to do with it and hopefully avoid getting more in the future.

Recognise spam

Spam is easy enough to recognise. It has subjects like 'Make $$$$$s fast', 'The ultimate win/win' and 'How to reinvent your life'. Spammers use computer programs to send millions of messages each day. They hope to catch at least a few gullible recipients from their effort. However, not all spam is as blatant; some of it can be quite friendly and chatty.

You may receive other commercial email which advertises legitimate products. These are likely to go to fewer people, perhaps targeting you because of some aspect of your buying profile. Nonetheless, you probably don't want this stuff either.

Email abuse and spam is a contentious topic. Most people on the receiving end want it controlled somehow and the senders claim the freedom to distribute it as their right. For them it's an incredibly cheap form of marketing.

Legislation is emerging in some countries to bring in some measure of control against abuse of an otherwise useful means of sales promotion. New technology is also helping to stop the tricks of those abusing the system. Until then you need to handle it yourself.

Delete spam with filters

Spammers use various tricks to disguise their identity. Sending back messages complaining or asking to be removed from their list usually doesn't work. The simplest thing for you to do is to delete it, without reading it. You don't think twice about throwing paper junk mail in the bin without reading it. This is the same type of thing. However, if you're getting a lot of spam, even deleting may be tedious. In that case, if you have filtering capability, the best thing is to set up an email filter to remove it.

Because of the way the bulk mailing programs work, bulk email is usually not addressed to you in person. Fortunately, this gives you a filtering criteria you can use to remove it. Use the filter to check if the recipient fields of an incoming message have your email address. If not, move it to a folder called 'Spam' or some other name you choose.

Some mail you do want to keep may not be personally addressed to you either, such as messages from company-wide mail groups and Internet mailing lists. If you receive these types of messages you need to set up filters to file them first and make the spam filter the last filtering criteria. In this way the spam filter only acts on messages that you don't want to read.

File the spam messages rather than deleting them, because every once in a while a normal message may end up in your 'Spam' folder. You can look in this folder occasionally, quickly scan the subject lines to find the good ones and move them, then delete everything else in the folder.

Consider other spam filtering options

Rather than the general spam filter described above, filters can be set up specifically to delete mail coming from known spamming sites. There are lists of these sites published on the Internet. However, the spammers just keep on moving, making this approach ineffective.

Various software products are available for filtering spam. These may be helpful, particularly if you don't have filtering capability. You must remember to keep these programs up to date so that the latest sites and methods of spammers are recognised.

If you use a corporate email system, you should also tell your email administrator that you are getting a lot of this rubbish. It may be possible to implement a filter for removing it before it reaches you. The email administrator may also have the expertise to go through the addressing information to find a suitable place to complain to.

Protect your email address

You may be wondering how the spammers obtained your email address. They have programs which read the messages sent to Internet mailing lists and extract the return email addresses. They pull addresses from World Wide Web pages. They take addresses from online email directories. They also buy mailing lists in much the same way as they could buy street address mailing lists.

When you fill out forms on the Web, some companies take this as an invitation to send you more advertising material and may even on-sell their list containing your address. So you can see that it's fairly easy for your address to be picked up and passed on. You can request for your name to be removed from online email directories. Apart from that, other than not using the Internet, there isn't a lot you can do about it.

To keep your work inbox clear, consider having a personal account for using the Internet and particularly for sending messages to Internet mailing lists. (There are some more ideas to protect your address when you are using Internet mailing lists given in Chapter 9.)

There's one other thing. Don't reply to spam, even to send a message asking to be removed from their list. Unscrupulous operators have been known to use removal requests as a means of validating that the address is 'live' and you get more, rather than less of it.

Register for spam if you want it

If you are one of the rare people who actually likes receiving copious amounts of advertising material, there are World

Wide Web sites where you can register your address and your product interests and you will receive it. These sites may even offer incentives to entice you to join up.

ORGANISING YOUR MAILER FOR PERSONAL EFFICIENCY

Another method for improving efficiency is to tailor your mailer so that it suits the way you work. You may be able to alter what is displayed. For example, you may be able to select which tools are on the toolbar and decide where the toolbar is displayed.

The example screen in Figure 4.4 is very different from the earlier examples. It uses the same mailer, but the screen layout has been changed to suit another person. It's worthwhile finding out what can be changed on your mailer and experimenting to get it just right for you.

Figure 4.4 Modified screen layout

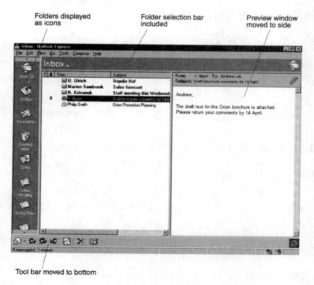

Folders displayed as icons

Folder selection bar included

Preview window moved to side

Tool bar moved to bottom

Your mailer is also likely to have settings which you can change to make it suit the type of messages you normally send and receive. Look for things like:

- Choosing 'Reply to all' or 'Reply to sender' as your normal reply option.
- Including or not including the original message in replies.
- How the address book operates, such as expanding nicknames into the real addresses as they are typed.
- Whether it keeps a copy of messages that you send.
- Which fonts are used and whether plain or formatted text is sent in the messages.
- The type of alert issued when new incoming mail is received.
- Automatic emptying of the trash folder on exit.
- How messages within the folders are sorted, such as by date or alphabetically by subject, so that they are easier for you to find.

MANAGING YOUR TIME

Time management is an important skill for anyone in business to master. For someone suffering from email overload, it's an essential skill. Basically, time management is about knowing your priorities and working to them. Here is a brief look at how you might begin to understand those priorities better.

Realise that you can't do it all

Perhaps the best place to start is recognising that you can't do it all. When you come to this simple conclusion, then you are ready to accept that you need to choose between the many things you could do to fill your day.

This leads you quite naturally to knowing that you should do the most important things, rather than occupying yourself with trivialities. Triviality could be reading and answering endless email messages on topics of little importance to you or your company. Triviality could be chatting to other people or tinkering with an unnecessary report instead of processing your email messages. So the crux of the issue seems to be: understand what's important.

Set your goals

To know what is genuinely important, you need to know what you are trying to achieve. You can do this by setting your goals. Spend a short time writing down the things you want to achieve. Try to make them specific and list the tasks that will lead you to each goal. Then look over your goals and activities and consider the following to help you decide which activities are top priority and which are of lesser importance:

- Which will benefit the company most?
- Which will I enjoy most?
- Which will help the most people?
- Which ones can be coordinated so that they help each other?
- Do any of them clash?

Prepare a daily schedule

Your activities will vary from day to day. To keep on track with your goals, keep a task list and from this prepare a daily schedule of activities. List the things you need to do today. Remember to look ahead to give yourself sufficient lead time for big tasks. Keeping your goals in mind, give each a priority. Plan to do the highest-priority activities first.

When you are processing your email messages, use your task list to select those you should act on fully today. Set aside others for action another day. However, keep those you set aside in an 'Action pending' folder or enter them into your activity schedule so they don't get forgotten.

Enhance your concentration

Try to schedule some quiet time in your day to get the big jobs done. No phone calls, no unnecessary talking and no running about. Do it at an appropriate time and place so that you can reduce interruptions, distractions and visitors.

Our email system is set up to check for new messages every ten minutes. I changed mine to every two hours but this upset the boss so I've compromised at one hour.

—Martin, Office Worker

You will find that focusing your concentration will help you to get more done. Similarly, settling down to an email session aimed at clearing the inbox is much more productive than handling messages randomly throughout the day. Your job and the way your company works will determine whether you need to check your inbox more than once a day.

If your company insists that you are always connected to email, then resist the urge to read every message as it arrives. You should be able to tell whether it's urgent from the subject.

Plan to clear your inbox every day

The idea of processing mail according to its importance is not advocating that you become lazy and allow your inbox to overflow with messages. Your aim should be to clear your inbox every day, otherwise it will get on top of you.

Remember to handle each message only once and exploit the filing and filtering tools to lift your productivity. Organise your mailer so that it works well for you. Assume responsibility for the way you answer and handle messages.

Start today. People delay because they're afraid of making a mistake. Some think it's not worth starting if they can't do it all. You can take it a step at a time. The important thing is to begin acting firmly.

MAKING PROGRESS

Tick off your daily tasks as each one is done. It will give you a sense of accomplishment and, very soon, you will act on your priorities with ease. You will find your whole day runs more smoothly and your email is completed more quickly.

Unfortunately, over time, the files you have been using to efficiently store your messages will begin to fill up. If you don't clean them up they'll eventually slow you down again. So you have another job to do.

The next chapter will help you to work out what to do with your filed messages. You'll understand what you can delete and what you must keep. You'll also learn how to find a message that is lost among all your other messages.

KEY POINTS

- Process each message only once by choosing to do one of the following:
  - Delete it.
  - Save it for reading or later action.
  - Pass it on.
  - Act on it.
- To set up an email filing system that works efficiently:
  - Review and revamp your current system.
  - Personalise your mailer.
  - Use filters to automatically file routine messages and remove unwanted mail.
  - Remember to put your filters in logical order.
- To manage your time:
  - Realise that you can't do it all.

> — Set your goals and prepare a daily schedule.
> — Work on enhancing your concentration.
> — Process your email messages according to your daily priorities.
> — Plan to clear your email inbox daily.

EXERCISES

Use these exercises to help you decide how to be more productive.

1. Read the list of Top Ten Time Wasters and underline the ones that apply to you.

    Top Ten Time Wasters
    1. Working on unimportant messages with low pay-off.
    2. Fragmenting your work. Jumping from message to message. Not handling each message only once.
    3. Not filing your messages, or using a poor filing scheme with an unproductive screen layout.
    4. Taking on work which belongs to others. Replying to everything yourself.
    5. Trying to process your email messages in an environment with distractions such as excessive noise, confusion or turmoil.
    6. Keeping too many messages and too much reading material.
    7. Writing too many email messages.
    8. Failing to ask or answer questions fully.
    9. Not making your mailer work for you with tools such as message filtering, the address book, templates and an automatic signature.

10. Having a loser's attitude. Believing there is nothing you can do to change things.

2. Using the items you have underlined as a guide, decide what you are going to change.

chapter 5

Can I use email messages for the record?

In the past, email was used only for transient conversations and transfer of working documents. This is changing as formal business is being transacted using email messages.

This chapter looks at issues arising from this change in usage. How do you find an old message among those you have stored in your email folders? What email messages do you need to keep? Is email a good place to keep them for the permanent record?

FINDING MESSAGES YOU WANT

When you save messages in your email folders, whether for the short term or the longer term, you need to be able to find them again. Fortunately, when you are looking for a particular message you usually have some clues about it. You may know who sent it, the approximate date it was sent, or some key words that will be in the subject or body of the message. Any of these will help you to find the message easily.

Figure 5.1 Setting search criteria

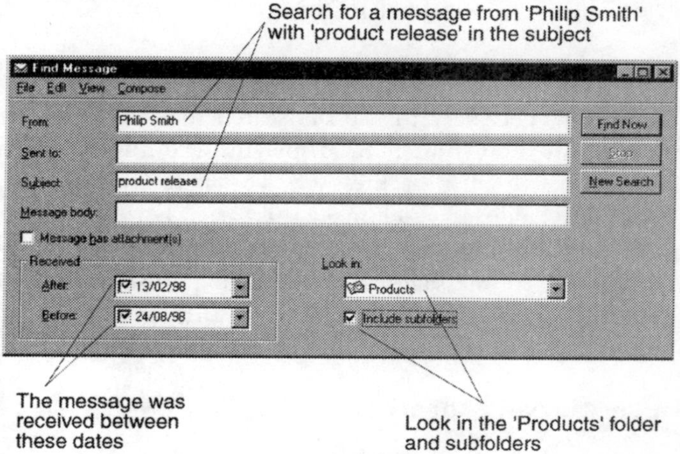

Search for a message from 'Philip Smith'
with 'product release' in the subject

The message was
received between
these dates

Look in the 'Products' folder
and subfolders

Use search criteria

Most mailers have a search facility. They will differ in the way
you specify what you are looking for and the search criteria
you can use. So you'll have to check what your mailer can
do.

Figure 5.1 shows the search window of a mailer. This
will search through the folders and subfolders looking for
messages that match the criteria and give a list of them to
select from.

Narrow your search

If you have a large number of messages, searching through all
of them could take some time. It's better to narrow the search
to the places where the message is likely to be found, as has
been done in the example above.

Your mailer will give you options to help you narrow the
search. It is unlikely that you will need to search all of your

messages to find what you are looking for, unless a message has been inadvertently filed in the wrong folder.

Scan the message list

It isn't always necessary to use the search tool to find a message. You can often find it by displaying the folder contents and scanning the list of messages yourself. Your mailer is likely to have facilities which make this easier. For example, you may be able to display the message list in alphabetical order by sender, so that all messages from the same person are grouped together. Alternatively, you could display them in date order so that you can skip to the approximate date quickly.

Display threads together

If you are chasing all of the correspondence relating to a particular subject, your mailer may also be able to help with this. Sorting the message list by conversation thread will list all of the messages with the same subject together. It will ignore 'Re:' and 'Fwd:' in front of the subject when it does this.

Displaying the list in this way will also help when you are cleaning up and want to delete duplicate correspondence or all messages relating to a completed task.

Know your search tools

Practise using the search tool and know how to change the way the message lists are sorted. After you have done this a few times, you'll have the skills ready to help you when you need to find an elusive message quickly.

WHAT MESSAGES DO YOU HAVE TO KEEP?

Many companies still treat email as a place where only transient things happen. It's true that most of the messages you are dealing with will probably have no lasting value. Therefore, it's important for you to identify any which do have longer-term significance and arrange for them to be kept securely.

Messages to keep

The following are the types of messages that you must keep for the longer-term record.

Business records. Messages that are used to transact business need to be kept for as long as their paper equivalent would be retained. For example, customer service records may have to be kept for a year, and purchasing records may have to be kept as evidence for the taxation authorities.

Legal records. Any messages recording legal obligations must be kept—for example, messages regarding contractual agreements. You should also keep all messages that may be needed as evidence in possible future legal proceedings.

Personnel records. Policy matters such as adopted work procedures are often distributed through email notification. A copy of these messages should be kept for the record.

Important messages. Some messages may be important to the business in that they could only be replaced at great cost and delay. If a message is considered to be important in this way, it should be kept and protected from loss.

When information that must be kept for the business record is being transmitted via email, responsibility for retaining the information should be specifically assigned. People tend to think of email as personal and are likely to give no consideration to keeping these records beyond their usefulness to themselves, unless they are instructed to do so.

Temporary messages

You will probably find that most of your records fall into the following temporary categories.

Transitory conversations. Notes about appointments, reminder messages, staff notices and such like can usually be deleted immediately.

Working notes. Working notes, such as questions and answers relating to a task and draft documents, are kept for reference until the task is complete and then they can be deleted. However, if your job requires you to justify the work done for billing purposes, then you will need to keep these messages as a longer-term record.

Short-term records. Similar to working notes, some messages form short-term records which are of little relevance once their time is past. For example, individual monthly sales forecasts need not be kept once the quarterly aggregate report has been prepared.

Reading and reference material. There will be some messages you want to keep for later reading or reference. A proportion of these messages will become out-of-date quite quickly, while others may have longer-term value but are unlikely to be useful for more than one or two years.

Personal messages. Personal messages are usually of temporary interest.

Duplicates

The nature of email means there are usually many duplicates of messages. Each person who receives a message has their own copy and the sender is likely also to have kept a copy. Further, a copy of the original message is often returned with the reply, so there are even more duplicates.

Clearly, there is no need for you to keep duplicates of messages you receive. For example, you can delete the message you sent as soon as you receive a reply with the original included.

Nor is there any reason for you to keep copies of messages when someone else has been assigned the job of keeping them for the formal record. However, if you are handling messages that you think should be kept, it would be wise to check that there is a person looking after their retention before you delete your copy.

CHOOSING HOW TO KEEP YOUR MESSAGES

For the many messages which are temporary in nature, your email folders are a fast and efficient way to store them for future use. For those that you have to keep for the longer term, you need to consider other methods. Here are some options:

- Print the message to be retained in a paper file.
- Retain the message in electronic form in another computer file.
- Retain the message as an email message.

Consider access by others

Before you make your decision on the form in which to keep messages, you need to think about their likely usage in the future. Are you the only person who needs to access these messages in the future, or are other people going to need them? If other people need the messages, then it's no good retaining them in your personal email folders.

Even if you are expected to be the only person who needs them, what happens if you change jobs? You are going to have to forward all of the messages to the person who takes over your old job. What happens if you leave the company? Often, email accounts are removed soon after people leave the company. That will make all of your stored messages inaccessible.

Retaining important messages in email doesn't look like a good prospect unless the information is stored in a shared folder that can be accessed by others.

Consider how long they have to be kept

How long does the record have to be kept? In just a few years, your current email system will almost certainly be obsolete. The fate of your stored messages depends on what type of upgrade is chosen. If a compatible email system is used, your stored messages could be automatically transferred into the new system. However, it's possible that this won't be the case. You will have to send each of the stored messages to the new email system or lose them.

So, if a message has to be kept for a long time (more than two years, say), storing it in email is not a good solution.

Consider your space limitations

There is rarely enough disk space for everyone to keep every message they want. So you need to consider whether there is enough disk space. Is it satisfactorily protected against disk failure? Is there a long-term retention policy for email messages? (To learn more about where your messages are stored and the limitations this may impose, read the section 'Understanding where your email messages are stored' at the end of this chapter.)

Choose a method

Given current technology and current work practices, email doesn't seem to be a good solution for long-term storage of business records. If it's important to retain the business record over many years, you should print it and file it in the appropriate paper filing system.

Alternatively, you could copy the message (or a group of related messages) and store it as a computer document. If your company has a system for electronic document management and archiving, this is a good choice because it has the added benefit of making the message easily accessible for other users. This choice is even better if your email system is integrated with a document management system.

HANDLING EXTRANEOUS CHATTER

When you are saving messages for the longer-term record, you may be concerned about extraneous chatter within messages which is of no value to the record. You can consider removing the extraneous information except when the records are going to be needed for legal purposes.

When the level of chatter is small, it's easy enough to ignore, so simply store it with the record. If it's large you may want to store edited highlights, indicating that this is what you have done. Remember, you must preserve the integrity of the record.

If, however, the sequence of events is important, as opposed to the final content, then you should store the complete messages. You may want to attach your own summary as quick guidance but leave the whole sequence of messages available should the reader need to investigate further.

To save a cut-down version of a message within email, make the changes and then send the message to yourself. You may also want to change the subject of a message to something that is more meaningful and easy to find. To do this, change the subject and send the message to yourself before filing it.

CLEANING UP YOUR MESSAGE FOLDERS

If you want to stay efficient you're going to have to clean up your folders every now and then. You're also going to have to do this to keep on the right side of storage space restrictions.

When the pressure is on you to clean up your message holdings, you need to be able to do it easily and quickly. You are much more likely to make mistakes and delete messages that you really meant to keep, if you let your folders grow bulky and out of control.

Don't plan on retrieving deleted messages

Retrieving inadvertently deleted messages is usually not easy. Some mailers will put deleted messages into a trash folder which will hold them where you can get them back, but once you clear the trash they are gone.

> *I have an 'Assist reps' folder where I store conversations with sales reps. I only occasionally have to go back to these messages. When I have to clean up in a hurry, I know I can delete the oldest messages from this folder without having to think or worry about what I might be deleting.*
>
> *—Michael, Product Manager*

Copies of messages are often kept so that the system can be recovered after disk failure or some similar disaster. Unfortunately, these are usually designed to recover all email messages. It often isn't possible to select an individual message and restore this.

You should therefore try to be calm and considered when you are doing bulk deletions of email messages. It's better to do regular clean-ups when you have time to think.

Only save messages you are going to need

The best way to keep your folders manageable is to not fill them with unnecessary clutter. If you won't need to refer to a message again, then don't file it. If you feel that you must keep it for a short while, put it in a 'Temporary messages' folder rather than mixing it up with other more permanent messages.

Delete duplicates as they occur

When a reply comes back to you with a copy of the original message, you now have two copies of the original message. You can save storage space if you delete the duplicate copy. You are more likely to do this if you establish a

> *I leave messages that are awaiting reply in the 'Sent items' folder. When the reply arrives, I delete the original message from the 'Sent items'. This gives me an easy way to clean up duplicates and also lets me know at a glance what replies are outstanding.*
>
> *—Antonia, Administrative Assistant*

procedure to delete the duplicate as soon as it occurs, rather than letting both copies end up in a folder to be cleaned up later.

Set a deletion date when you save messages

Some mailers allow you to set a deletion date when you save messages. This is a good way to have clean-ups occurring without you having to think about them.

Organise yourself for easy clean-up

When you devise your filing system, keep clean-up in mind. For example, if you know a project has a limited lifespan, keep messages relating to this in the one folder. When the project is finished, you can simply delete the whole folder.

If a message has to be kept for the permanent record, put it in a special folder, or group of folders, specifically for this type of message. Don't intermix important messages with more temporary messages.

Remember, you want to handle messages as few times as possible, preferably only once. If it's a message that has to end up in the paper files, print it at the time you save it so the job is done. If it has to be saved as a document elsewhere, do it straight away. If you won't need the message again once

> *Our email system has a default deletion date of three months. Any message I keep will be automatically deleted three months later, unless I specifically change the retention date to keep the mail for longer.*
>
> —*Michelle, Office Worker*

it has been filed elsewhere, then delete it rather than saving it.

Plan regular clean-ups

Experts estimate that 95 per cent of all filed materials over a year old are never referred to again. Therefore, a lot of messages in your folders can probably be deleted. Planning ahead makes the task of cleaning up much easier. You will know which folders contain messages you can delete without concern.

There will be other folders which have a mixture of outdated and useful messages. Every once in a while, go through a couple of folders and remove outdated messages. You can probably tell from the subject alone whether the material is no longer useful, so the task doesn't need to be onerous.

UNDERSTANDING WHERE YOUR EMAIL MESSAGES ARE STORED

You may not be able to keep all of the messages that you would like to keep. To know how many messages you can keep and how long you can keep them, you need to understand where your email messages are stored. This involves a short technical explanation.

The email server and email client

The computer system which receives and holds your email messages until you are ready to read them is called the *email server*. When you start your mailer, it connects to your email server and collects any messages that are waiting for you on the server. This is why mailers are also known as *email clients*.

In a corporate environment, the email server is usually a computer which is owned and managed by the company. All of the email users in a building typically connect to the one email server. Email servers are often connected together so that messages can be easily sent to people throughout the company, regardless of where they are located.

A company's email server may also be connected to the Internet. Messages coming from outside the company are delivered to this server. If there is no Internet connection, you can only send and receive messages from people within your company.

In a small office environment, or when you use a personal email account at home, the email server is provided and managed by your *service provider*. Messages for you are sent to this server. When you are ready to process your email messages, you connect your mailer (via the telephone) to the service provider's email server.

Messages can be stored at the client or server

Messages are temporarily stored at the email server until your mailer, the client, reads them. Whether they remain at the server for long-term storage depends on your email system.

When you use a corporate email system, your mailer usually reads your messages from the server and leaves them at the server. When you create folders, they are created at the server. When you move messages to the folders, these are stored at the server. The disk where your messages are being stored is at the email server, not at your desktop computer.

When you use a service provider, this is different. Your mailer reads the messages from the service provider's server. When the messages have been successfully sent to your mailer, the mailer usually deletes them from the server. The messages are now kept by your mailer. When you create folders, they are created on the disk at your desktop. When you move messages to folders, this is done on the disk at your desktop. Some corporate email systems also work in this way.

Other email systems let you choose where a message is to be stored—at the server, at the desktop or at both.

When messages are stored at the server

When your messages are stored at the server, copies for protection against disaster (called a *back-up*) are made by your email administrator. In the event of disaster, such as a disk failure, the email administrator will restore the messages. This saves you having to worry about making back-ups.

There is usually a large number of users sharing the server and the server has a finite amount of disk space. Because of this, the email administrator often imposes restrictions on the amount of disk storage each user can use. This will affect the total number of messages you can save in your folders. If you are given just a small amount of disk space, you won't be able to keep many messages for long-term storage in email.

Sometimes, the disk storage restriction isn't imposed on individual users but on the group as a whole. In this case, you are likely to receive occasional messages from the email administrator urging you to clean up your email messages to make room on the server disk for new messages. Again, you may be restricted in the number of messages you can keep.

Be aware that some email administrators take a high-handed attitude in trying to manage this communal disk space. For example, they may decide to delete all messages that are more than a year old. Hopefully, they will warn you before they do it so that you can transfer any critical messages to another place. This type of policy will influence whether you use email for long-term storage of your messages.

When messages are stored at the client

When messages are stored at the client desktop, the number of messages you can store will be determined by the amount of disk space you have available on your desktop computer. The messages are also not backed up by an email administrator. Back-up is your responsibility. (If you are in a corporate environment, there may be an established procedure for backing up desktop disk files.) It is essential to have a suitable back-up and restoration procedure if you are going to use email to hold critical business records.

BEING AWARE OF THE RISKS ASSOCIATED WITH EMAIL RECORDS

This chapter has stated that people tend to think of email as personal. When it comes to setting up the mailer, filing messages and choosing which ones to delete, all of these choices are personal.

As more formal business is transacted by email, it becomes less of a personal tool. However, this business information is usually side-by-side with messages that are truly personal. This raises questions about the privacy of your email messages and the right of your employer to have access to your messages. The next chapter explains how secret and personal your email really is.

KEY POINTS

- To find a message quickly, use your mailer's search tool.
  - Narrow the search to folders where the message is most likely to be.

- — Sort your message lists in an order that helps you to scan for the messages more easily.
- There are different types of email messages:
  - — Most email messages are temporary, such as transitory conversations and working notes.
  - — Some have to be kept longer or never destroyed, such as business and legal records.
  - — There will often be duplicates. Only one copy needs to be kept.
- When choosing to keep messages:
  - — Consider whether others need to access them. Email is usually unsuited to this.
  - — Consider how long they have to be held. Email is unsuited to long-term storage.
  - — Consider how much disk space you have available to store messages. There is often not enough to keep a lot of messages.
  - — If it isn't to be stored in email, then print it or save it as a computer file.
  - — Be careful to maintain the integrity of the record if you choose to remove extraneous email chatter from the information that is stored.
- You can make cleaning up your folders easier if you:
  - — Only save messages you are going to need again and set a deletion date when you save them.
  - — Delete duplicates as they occur.
  - — Keep messages of short lifespan in folders separate from messages needing longer-term storage.
  - — Plan regular clean-ups.

EXERCISES

In these exercises you review how you are going about the longer-term management of your email messages.

1. **Do you handle any of these types of messages?**
   ☐ Business records
   ☐ Legal records
   ☐ Personnel records
   ☐ Important messages
   ☐ Working notes needed to justify work for billing purposes.

   Are you keeping these messages? If not, is someone else doing it? Is the method you are using suitable for long-term storage?

2. **Are your folders organised to make cleaning up easy?**
   Decide on any improvements you could make.

chapter 6

Are my email messages secret?

Email can be intimate and personal, lulling you into a cosy sense of privacy. This is a false feeling—your email isn't secret. Nor should you be fooled into thinking snoops won't harm you because it would involve exposing their own unsavoury activities. The matter of email privacy is complex and more wide-reaching than mere good manners or your potential embarrassment.

WHY YOUR EMAIL MESSAGES CAN BE READ BY OTHERS

You need to know what could happen to your messages and how you can protect yourself. In the corporate environment, in particular, there are good reasons for people other than you having access to your email messages. Here are some of them.

The email administrator has to protect them

You would be very annoyed if one day your email system lost all of your email messages and the email administrator couldn't get them back again. To protect against this eventuality, duplicate copies of messages are taken regularly and stored in a safe place. To have the power to do this also gives the administrator the power to see every message.

Other computers have information about your messages

To reach its destination your message has potentially gone through several other computers, so information about it is now dispersed all over the place.

Further, while the message is in transit over a network, snoops can tap in and take a look. Maybe the snoop is a thief who sells company information; perhaps it's a voyeur or the office gossip. All are possibilities.

Monitoring programs can read your messages

To assist in system management there are often computer programs for monitoring message activity. These can produce a plethora of details about email messages and can be readily used to eavesdrop on employee activity.

DELETING DOESN'T GET RID OF YOUR MESSAGES

As if all of these potential points of exposure weren't enough, deleting your message doesn't actually dispose of it for all time. Many of the copies taken to protect your message remain in back-up storage, ready to be retrieved by someone in the future who wants to know what you were up to.

DOES IT MATTER THAT YOUR MESSAGES CAN BE READ?

You are probably now convinced that there is some lack of privacy in your email messages. However, you may argue that even though your messages could be read, no one would bother reading them. You may think that if they did, you could take action against them because they don't have the right to invade your privacy.

The law of email varies from country to country and is only just evolving. However, there are a couple of cases that went to court in the United States that you can learn from.

Don't believe it won't be done

The case of *Flanagan et al. v Epson America, Inc.* shows that employers have been known to monitor email. Alana Shoars, the email administrator at Epson, was horrified to discover her supervisor reading and printing electronic mail messages between other employees. During training sessions she had assured users that their email was private and now she found a manager betraying that trust. After questioning the practice she found herself fired for insubordination.

Shoars filed a class-action suit on behalf of herself and other employees, claiming invasion of privacy. She lost her claim, which was based on a wire-tapping statute and California's constitution.

The court decision ruled that email was not covered by the wire-tapping statute and that the constitutional right to privacy covered personal, not business information.

Bad-mouthing the boss can really hurt you

The case of *Michael A. Smyth v The Pillsbury Company* shows that bad-mouthing the management by email is a risky thing to do. Michael Smyth was fired for making inappropriate and unprofessional comments after an email he sent to a co-worker was intercepted. He had called his managers 'backstabbing bastards', along with other comments.

Despite repeated assurances by Pillsbury to their staff that email messages were private, the court dismissed Smyth's claim that he was wrongfully terminated based on a violation of his privacy.

The court ruled that they did not find a reasonable expectation of privacy in email communications voluntarily made by an employee over the company email system despite any assurances that such communications would not be intercepted by management. They also considered that the company's interest in preventing inappropriate and unprofessional comments or illegal activity over its email system outweighed any privacy interest of the employee.

Your employer owns the system and the messages

It seems to come down to this: your employer owns the system and therefore owns the messages on it, even those which are entirely personal. Further, in some cases, promises by your employer that they won't examine your email may prove worthless.

OTHER SITUATIONS THAT CAN LEAD TO EMAIL DISCLOSURE

Disclosure of email messages can result from more than just someone being nosy. Here are some of the other situations that can lead to email disclosure.

Concern for business detriment

An employer may be looking for evidence of activities that are perceived to be detrimental to the business, like in the case where a Borland International vice president was accused of disclosing confidential information in email messages to a competitor, Symantec. The messages were searched for and discovered in the archived files after the executive had left Borland to join Symantec.

Employers can also be concerned about employees running outside businesses and doing other inappropriate activities via the company's email system.

Freedom of information

Government employees should expect that their email messages are subject to freedom of information legislation, in just the same way as paper records. To support this legislation, government bodies have a responsibility to archive messages for long-term storage.

Email messages sent within the context of government are usually only private until someone asks about them.

Legal discovery

When the court is gathering the facts to decide a case, email messages can be subpoenaed, discovered and intercepted under law. Experts may even be called to recover archived and deleted files.

The law does have guidelines which restrict the level of disclosure. For example, only relevant messages can be admitted as evidence. However, a situation which is entirely unrelated to you may result in strangers looking through your messages to find what is relevant.

Getting the job done

Setting aside these more heavy-handed possibilities, in the workplace there is the ordinary matter of getting the job done. There is sometimes a need to get into the files of other people because they are away or the unexpected has happened.

As with paper files and desk drawers, there is always the possibility that this may reveal something you would have preferred to have remained private. Given that we don't expect the unexpected, this has always been a risk.

Misaddressed mail

Not all mail gets delivered properly. An incorrect address could send your message to the wrong person, who can read it and possibly misuse it. Also, when a message is returned undelivered it is sometimes sent to the email administrator who can't help but see your message.

Someone passes it on

There's always the possibility of a message that you thought to be private between you and another person being passed on by that person to others. That is a risk you take with every message.

Hacker attack

Finally, there could be people intent on reading your company's mail for mischievous or malicious purposes. These people are known as computer hackers or crackers. Your internal communication could have high commercial value when in the wrong hands. It makes it worth their effort to view all the messages.

FALSIFICATION OF EMAIL HAPPENS TOO

The mention of hackers warns of another possibility—the misuse of your email address. A hacker could tamper with your email message during its transfer between computers. Hackers have become very sophisticated in their methods of activity. They can also send messages from their own address purporting to be from your address.

The more likely risk, however, is someone sending a

message from your computer because you have left it unat-
tended with your mailer open. It may be very difficult for
you to prove you didn't send the message yourself.

You may not even find out about the message being sent,
even though numerous people may be hurting and thinking
unkind thoughts about you as a result of a falsified message.
People tend to trust the technology and don't even conceive
of it being misused by someone impersonating you.

DIGITAL SIGNATURES AND ENCRYPTION CAN HELP

A *digital signature* helps to protect against message falsification
and tampering. It's a form of electronic signature which shows
that you wrote the message and it hasn't been tampered with.
Encryption can prevent your messages being read by people other
than those to whom they were sent. Here is how they work.

Public key encryption

Encryption is a process of encoding a message so that it is
scrambled and cannot be read except by a person who has
the key for decoding the message. Another person can possibly
decode the message, but this is extremely difficult as well as
taking a huge amount of computing power.

Public key encryption uses a matched pair of encryption and
decryption keys. Each person has a private key and a public
key. A message scrambled with the public key can only be
unscrambled with the matching private key. So, if you want
to send an encrypted message to a person, you will encrypt it
using their public key. Only the person you intend to read the
message will be able to do so, because they are the only person
with the private key needed to decrypt the message.

To send messages to you, people will obtain your public
key, encrypt their messages using this key and send them to

you. You will be the only person able to read the messages because you are the only one with the private key that matches the public key that was used to encrypt the messages.

When I receive encrypted messages, my email system automatically decrypts them using my private key. To me it's just like reading ordinary email messages.

—Kim, Business Executive

If a message goes astray, is intercepted in transit or is seen by the email administrator, it will appear as scrambled characters that are totally unreadable. You are the only person with the key to reading it.

Digital signatures

The encryption keys can be used in the opposite direction. Something encrypted using your private key can only be decrypted using your public key. Because your public key has successfully decrypted it, then it must have been sent by you because you are the only person who has the private key. This is used to create a digital signature.

A digital signature doesn't encrypt the message. It encrypts just a special signature component which can be used to prove you sent the message and that the message hasn't been tampered with.

Digital signatures are automatically interpreted by the mailer and it will inform you if the result shows that the message has been compromised. If your mailer can't interpret digital signatures and you receive a digitally signed message, you will still be able to read the message. You just won't have the assurance offered by the signature.

Messages can be both digitally signed and encrypted.

Digital certificates

To be able to use a digital signature and encryption, you need encryption keys. Your encryption software may generate these for you or they may be provided by your network security administrator or a commercial certifying authority. A commercial certifying authority guarantees their *digital certificate* has been granted to people who are really who they claim to be.

The keys are long and complicated. Fortunately, you don't have to remember them. Your own keys are stored on a file on the hard disk of your computer.

You can obtain a person's public key from the World Wide Web site of the certifying authority or other public directories on the Internet. Alternatively, you can ask the person to send you a digitally signed message. This will include their public key which you can then store in your address book.

When you obtain your own key file you should make sure you make a back-up copy of it in case your hard disk fails. Your key file cannot be replaced and you will need it to read encrypted messages. The key file is protected using a password. This may be a special encryption password or the password that is used to gain access to your computer.

Use S/MIME for easy encryption

In the past, digital signatures and encryption have required the two parties to have similar email set-ups (such as having the same mailer and encryption software installed). In recent times a method has been developed to allow disparate email systems to communicate securely. This is called Secure/MIME or *S/MIME*. S/MIME uses public key encryption technology.

It is expected that S/MIME will be widely implemented, which will make it easy for people to send encrypted messages to each other, even if they have different mailers.

Considerations when using encryption

Encryption methods that use longer keys are more secure because they are extremely difficult to decode without the encryption key.

The US government restricts the export of this technology because there is concern about encryption being used to hide criminal activities (a concern mirrored in other countries). This may restrict use of encryption in your country to less secure versions.

> *My management is so suspicious. If I started encrypting my messages, they would jump to the conclusion I have something to hide.*
>
> *—Connie, Research Engineer*

Encryption may do you more damage than having your correspondence read. Even if you have the ability to encrypt messages, it may not always be wise to do so. On the other hand, if your company is transferring sensitive commercial information via email, encryption may be actively encouraged to protect it.

WHAT ELSE YOU CAN DO TO PROTECT YOUR MESSAGES

Encryption may help to keep your email secret, but it isn't the only thing that can be done. Let's look at what else you can do to protect yourself from unpleasant incidents as a result of your email address being abused or your private email messages being read.

Protect your password

The most important thing for you to do is to protect your mailer from access by people other than you. This is the most vulnerable point in email security.

Have you ever left your desk with the mailer still signed on? Someone could have sat at your desk and read your mail or, even worse, sent a nasty message using your address.

Is your password easy to guess by knowing just a little bit about you? Someone could gain access to your mailer by trying simple things like the names of your children, your car registration or your nickname.

Have you told someone else your password or left it written in a place that's easy to find? You risk having someone access your email without your knowledge. Here are some things you can do to keep your password more secure:

- Change your password frequently.
- Don't use passwords that are easily associated with you, such as your nickname.
- Make your password more complicated by putting in different symbols, like * and #.
- Don't share your password.
- If someone knows your password, change it.
- Close down your mailer when you leave your desk. If your computer allows you to lock the keyboard, you can use this instead.

People have been tricked into giving their password to strangers who have then used it to gain access to the company records. For example, someone pretends to be from the help desk and asks you questions, one of which is your password, under the pretext of needing it to change your set-up. If they were authorised to do this work, they wouldn't need your password.

Remember, your password is like your signature. It gives access to everything that is done from your email address. Messages sent from your email address will be attributed to you, even if you didn't send them. Your password may even give access to your private encryption key which would allow the impostor to digitally sign the messages as well.

Think twice before you send

You should work on the assumption that every email message you send is an open document that could end up with the person you'd least like to see it. Ordinary message forwarding and human errors can spread it about without any need for complicated monitoring and prying by anyone.

Even if you use encryption, once it is decrypted by the recipient it can be printed and passed on. So you still need to think about the message content of encrypted messages. If you are careful about what you write and send, you can greatly reduce any risk of embarrassment.

Know your company's email policy

Find out if your company has a published policy with regard to email privacy. Also check if there is a statement about the use of your email address for non-business use. You should operate within these guidelines.

Many companies are prepared to ignore a low level of personal use but will investigate if someone appears to be wasting company resources and time with a lot of personal messages. Respect the privilege of having an email address supplied to you. If your personal usage is going to be high, you should arrange to get a personal email address.

> *The policy in our company states: 'Email is a company resource that isn't to be used for personal messages.' I take this to mean they reserve the right to read our messages, since none are supposed to be personal.*
>
> *—Sergio, Accountant*

It can be assumed that you don't have privacy rights unless your employer gives you those rights. These rights can be given explicitly through a policy statement or implicitly through a course of conduct over years. Even if these rights are stated, you should still be wary of them. Companies are beginning to publish email usage and privacy policies. Most, however, state that the facility is for business use, with no commitment to personal privacy.

Respect the privacy of others

Do to others as you would have them do to you. Don't forward any email messages that may cause distress or embarrassment to the original sender. Don't pry into the email of other people. This includes not reading messages that are at the printer waiting to be collected. Remember to pick up your own printouts promptly, just in case others are not as respectful of your privacy.

TREAT EMAIL LIKE A POSTCARD

It is said that email messages are more like a postcard than a letter. Just like a postcard, an email message can be read by anyone who handles it and may end up being pinned to the office noticeboard for everyone to read. You need to think of your messages as having this level of openness even when encryption is used.

Encryption is an emerging area for email and you can expect to see it used more widely in future as S/MIME is beginning to make it easier for different mailers to handle encrypted messages. S/MIME is a new version of MIME. In the next chapter you will learn about attachments. You will find there that MIME has already made it much easier for attached documents to be handled by different mailers.

KEY POINTS

- Your email can be read by others for back-up purposes and monitoring.
  - Deleting your messages doesn't necessarily delete back-up copies.
- Legal cases have established that email messages belong to your employer if your employer has provided the computer system.

- There are many things that can lead to disclosure of an email message, including:
  - Employer concerns about business detriment.
  - Freedom of information requests to government bodies.
  - Legal discovery.
  - Collaboration in the workplace to get the job done.
  - Mail being misaddressed and read by the wrong person.
  - A valid recipient passing on the message to someone else.
  - Hacker attack.
- Email messages can be falsified by someone:
  - Tampering with them during transfer.
  - Purporting to be you by using your email address.
- A digital signature can be used to verify that you sent the message and that it hasn't been tampered with.
- Encryption can be used to scramble a message so that only the valid recipient can read it. You should also:
  - Protect your password from misuse.
  - Only send messages you are happy for others to read.
  - Know your company's email policies and work within these guidelines.
  - Treat all email messages, even encrypted ones, as being potentially open to being read by others.

EXERCISES

In these exercises you review your expectations of email privacy and how well you manage your own email security.

1. **Obtain a copy of your company's email policy.**
   If there isn't one, see if there are any accepted work practices and understandings about email use and privacy. Read the policy carefully. Are you surprised by anything in it? Will knowing this policy influence the way you use email in the future?

2. **Test how security-aware you are by ticking the boxes below which apply to you. Do you:**
   ☐ Change your password frequently?
   ☐ Have a password that isn't easily associated with you?
   ☐ Have a password that is more complicated than a simple word?
   ☐ Keep your password secret?
   ☐ Close down your mailer (or lock the keyboard) before you leave your desk?

   The more ticks the better. For any you haven't ticked, what are you going to do to reduce this security exposure? Now go back and tick all of the boxes so that your security exposures aren't revealed.

chapter 7

Help, I can't read the attachments!

One of the really useful aspects of email is being able to send all kinds of documents to other people. Unfortunately, delight can turn into great consternation when the people at the other end don't seem able to read the document you've sent. The primary reason for these difficulties is incompatibility between the two computers.

Over many years, software designers have developed methods for different email systems to communicate successfully. Older mailers may not handle the most recent methods which have made document handling much easier. Understanding a little about these methods and the way attachments work may help you to resolve any difficulties you're having in transferring documents to other people.

HOW YOU KNOW THERE IS AN ATTACHMENT

The first clue about how your attachments work is in the way they are displayed by your mailer. Attachments are usually displayed in one of two ways.

They will often be displayed with an icon for the attached

Figure 7.1 A message with an attachment

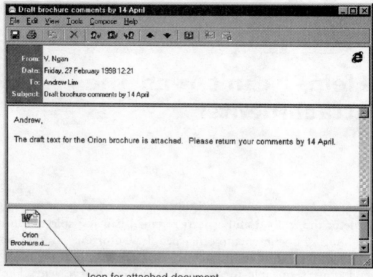

Icon for attached document

document and the document name, something like in Figure 7.1. In some cases the document name is simply displayed in the header. The actual contents of the document are occasionally also displayed within the message.

The other way attachments appear is as garbled characters following the text of the message, something like the example below. Don't despair—it may still be possible to make sense of an attachment like this.

How an attachment may look

```
q3S*W@Wi9AtDjjG,lo.FE9T)+EZc+Du+8FWbla0JGXG+Eo
&MD..B+ME"VYG3tGjloKlwFg+rRstgTgH
ehJUhyTGf$5^7dlb I RVBgghjheopbjeljeH&0PkIMNig
ergbidfUhr%36ghbinylkfg;jhghoJehvnhg
&9ARfgFHNMIpJK?2HP;JLQE+*cq4aM!|AkYt
```

A process called encoding and decoding is used to transfer attachments. Most mailers today encode and decode automatically. However, if yours displays garbled characters like in the example above or you are getting error messages about encoding, then read the section 'Encoding and decoding attachments' at the end of the chapter to find out what to do.

WHY ATTACHMENTS CAN'T BE READ

Unfortunately, having a decoded attachment doesn't mean all your potential problems are solved. Here are some other things that may be preventing you from reading an attachment.

Do you have the application program?

You need the right application program to be able to read the attachment. If the attached file is a word-processed document, then you need a word-processing program. If it is a spreadsheet, then you need a spreadsheet program and so on.

You have to start the required application program to open the file. Use the 'Open' command, or when there's an icon displayed you can simply double-click on it. If all goes well, the correct application program will be launched and the file opened ready for you to read.

When the particular application program required isn't installed on your computer, then it won't be able to start. For example, the document may have been created

> *When I am unable to read a file, I talk to the sender to see if their application can save the file in a format that my application can read. We can usually work something out.*
>
> —*Marco, Product Manager*

using a different word-processing program from the one you use. In this case, save the attachment as a file using the menu commands. Then start the required application program and see if it's possible to open the file from within the application. Alternatively, the application may let you import the file.

Word processors often have options which allow files to be saved in the format of other word processors, or if none of these match, you could try rich text format or text only format. Other types of programs, such as spreadsheets, presentation and graphics programs, also allow their files to be saved in other formats.

Do you have the right version?

Even though you have the same application program that the sender used, you could still have trouble reading the attachment if your program is a different version level. If the sender has a later version than yours, your application program is unlikely to read the document. The sender may be able to save the file in the format of the older version, and then you should have no trouble reading the file.

Is the document too large?

There are often limits on the size of the email messages a server can receive. If you are trying to read an attachment that's too large for the server, you will probably get an error message saying the attachment has been truncated or rejected.

To solve this problem see if the sender can compress the attachment with a compression program or break the attachment into smaller pieces and send it as several messages. Some mailers have facilities for doing this automatically.

Are there other incompatibilities?

It's possible that other issues and inconsistencies are preventing you from reading the attachment. Differences between the sender's computer and your computer can cause problems.

If you're still having trouble after eliminating the likely causes, you may need someone with deeper technical understanding to help you. There is also the possibility that the attachment is getting corrupted during transfer.

> *Even after we managed to get the attachments transferring properly, our branch offices still couldn't read them. They had an older operating system which couldn't handle long file names.*
>
> —*Sarah, System Analyst*

WHEN YOU ARE SENDING ATTACHMENTS

Modern mailers have made it very easy to transfer attachments in email messages and many users have modern mailers. Therefore, it's probably easiest to assume that transferring the attachment is going to work. If it doesn't work, then you can try to eliminate the problems.

Ask if they can handle attachments

You might like to send a simple query asking if the recipient can accept attachments easily. Send something like the message below. Then the recipient can respond letting you know what problems have occurred in the past.

▨ A query about attachments

Julie,
I can email the floor plans when they are ready. Can you handle attachments?

Understand size limitations by comparison

People may know that their server has message size limitations. However, it's sometimes difficult to understand what

64K or 1Mb or 10Mb really means. It can be easier to express it in terms of the types of documents they have been able to receive successfully in the past. The response to the earlier query could be something like this:

▨ Response to query about attachment

Roger,
I can handle attachments but it seems to baulk at really big ones. Jason managed to send wiring diagrams so I think the floor plans will get through OK.

Ask about the software application

Even if sending the attachments works like a charm, it's not going to be any use to the recipients if they don't have the right program to read or view the file. You could send a query something like this:

▨ A query about software

Julie,
I'm ready to send the diagram for the new floor layout. I can save it in bmp, eps, jpg or tif format. Which would you prefer?

Alternatively, when you are fairly sure the recipient has the right software, you could just send the attachment together with a note telling them what software and version level you used. They will get back to you if they can't read it.

OTHER THINGS TO CONSIDER WITH ATTACHMENTS

There are several other things that you should consider when you are sending and receiving documents.

Only use attachments when you must

For some users reading an attachment can be an annoying process involving a lot of steps. It's much easier to read a normal email message. So, as a general rule, if the information can be sent as a straightforward message then do so.

Still use attachments for very long documents; for documents that have formatting (bold, italic, tables and such) that you don't want to lose; and for specialist documents such as presentations, diagrams and spreadsheets.

Include your email address in the document

When the attachment is printed or saved as a file it becomes disassociated from the covering email message. To help your readers get back to you, it's a good idea to include your email address in the document itself.

Beware of viruses

Computer viruses which can corrupt your computer system may be passed in documents. You should treat all outside documents as potentially suspect and have a virus checker verify that they are clean before you use them. Your computer system may be set up to do this automatically, sometimes at the server before it even reaches you. If you don't know, confirm this with your system administrator.

HANDLING ATTACHMENTS AS A REMOTE USER

Remote users usually have a slow link to the email server. This includes people working from home on dial-up lines. Transferring large attachments can be very slow for these people as they wait for the file to be transferred from the server to their computer via the slow link. If you think your recipient will be accessing your message using a slow link, ask before you send a large attachment to them.

If you work remotely, see if your mailer has a facility for leaving messages at the server and displaying the message size. Some can even be set up to warn you when a message is large. Using these indicators you can then choose to leave big messages at the server unread when you are connected remotely. Later, when you are on a faster link, you can process the larger messages. If you are always on a slow link, use these methods so that you can leave reading the big messages to a more convenient time.

COPYRIGHT CONSIDERATIONS WITH ATTACHMENTS

Copyright restrictions apply to any documents that you attach to your email messages. You need to think of copyright, particularly when you are posting messages on public mailing lists. There is more chance that you may inadvertently over-step the mark with attachments than in a simple email message.

Copyright laws vary from country to country, so it's only possible to give some general guidelines here. Ask your legal adviser if you are unsure. Copyright rules are based on the idea of 'fair use'. Fair use allows you to use a small amount of a publication without seeking permission. For example, you can safely quote a few lines or a couple of paragraphs from a large publication. Quoting the same amount from a short poem would be another matter. You could be infringing copyright if you include any of the following without permission:

- More than three paragraphs in succession or quoting from the same publication more than five or six times.
- More than one line of a poem or song.

- Anything that is complete and copyrightable in itself, such as a photograph, a map or a cartoon.

ENCODING AND DECODING ATTACHMENTS

This section explains what is going on behind the scenes when attachments are being transferred. It will help you if you are having problems with encoding and decoding attachments.

Email was originally designed to send plain text characters only. The problem is that attached documents usually contain characters that aren't plain text. To be able to send the attachment safely from one computer to the next, the attachment has to be changed to plain text.

Encoding

Converting the attachment into plain text uses a process called *encoding*. A computer program reads the attachment and does the encoding. Once the attachment has been encoded it can be added to the rest of the email message and sent successfully.

While the encoded attachment consists of plain text characters, it doesn't look like ordinary words. It looks like garbled characters.

Decoding

When the attachment is received, it has to be converted back to what it was originally. This uses a process called *decoding*. A computer program reads the text and decodes it back into a readable file.

To decode an attachment, you need the decoding program that matches the encoding program. If you try to decode using the wrong program, you'll get garbage instead of a readable file.

Modern mailers encode and decode automatically. However, if you have one that shows attachments as garbled characters within the message, you'll have to do it manually.

Automatic encoding and decoding with MIME

The most commonly used encoding and decoding program today is called *MIME* (which stands for Multipurpose Internet Mail Extensions). If you have a MIME-compliant mailer, it automatically encodes outgoing messages into MIME format and decodes incoming messages that are in MIME format (and in other common encoding formats).

If you don't have a MIME-compliant mailer and people are sending messages to you in MIME format, you will be able to read the body of the message but not the attachment. You may be able to obtain a MIME decoding program which will let you read the attachment.

Automatic encoding and decoding without MIME

Your mailer may still encode and decode attachments automatically but using something other than MIME. To be able to send and receive attachments successfully without MIME, you will have to speak with the other person and find which encoding and decoding programs you can use. One of you may have a mailer which allows you to select different options and hopefully you can find a match, otherwise one of you may have to use manual encoding. Typically the different computer platforms (PC, Macintosh, Unix) have their own favoured versions. There are some, such as uuencode, which work across different platforms.

When you're sending email messages with attachments to other people within your company or people using the same network, you should be able to handle them easily without any fuss about MIME, encoding or decoding. Because the same mailers are used, they will both use the same type of encoding and be able to process attachments automatically.

Manual encoding and decoding

To encode and decode manually, you use an encoding/decoding program that runs separately from your mailer. The program you use must encode and decode a format that both you and the recipient can handle. Find out what programs are available to you (there are shareware versions available) and speak with the other person to see if there is something that you can both use.

To send an attachment using manual encoding:

1. Run the encoding program against the document you want to attach. The program will create an output file.
2. Copy the contents of the output file and paste it into your email message. It will appear as a lot of garbled characters.
3. Send the message.

To decode an attachment manually:

1. Save the message as a file using the 'Save as' option of your mailer.
2. Run the matching decoding program against this file. The output file created by the program will be a decoded document ready for you to read.

WHEN ALL ELSE FAILS . . .

Difficulties associated with reading attachments can be complex because of the many potential factors involved. It's only possible to give you a basic framework here that may help you in troubleshooting the problem. If you systematically look at each of the items described in this chapter, you will generally have success or at least know why you can't succeed. If all else fails, you will have to revert to old methods like posting a floppy disk or faxing the document.

This chapter has looked at one of the very useful areas of email which unfortunately sometimes involves you with technical issues to get it to work. The next chapter looks at an assortment of other features and topics, both technical and practical, that have not yet been covered in this book, such as HTML stationery, automatic forwarding and alternative email services.

KEY POINTS

- Attachments are encoded for safe transfer across the network.
    - They must be decoded with a matching program at the receiving end.
    - MIME-compliant mailers and some others do this automatically.
- Reasons attachments can't be read are:
    - Not having the right decoding program.
    - Not having an application program that can read the file.
    - Not having the right version of the application program.
    - The document is too big.
    - Other incompatibilities.
- Other things to consider are:
    - Not using attachments unless they are necessary.
    - Including your email address in the attached document.
    - Scanning incoming documents for viruses.
    - Remembering the copyright laws.

EXERCISES

These exercises guide you towards sending and receiving attached documents successfully.

1. **Have you had a problem with reading attachments?**
    Which of the following is the likely cause?
    ☐ Not having the right decoding program.
    ☐ Not having an application program that can read the file.
    ☐ Not having the right version of the application program.
    ☐ The document is too big.
    ☐ Other issues.
    Try to resolve the problem using the suggestions in this chapter.

2. **Does your email server have size restrictions on messages?**
    Given this restriction, what types of documents are you unlikely to be able to receive?

3. **Are you sure that documents that are sent to you as attachments are being automatically scanned by a virus checker?**
    If not, find out how to activate the virus checker.

chapter 8

What other clever things can I use?

Are your email messages plain and without character? Do you have trouble handling your email when you travel? Have you ever received a message like this and wondered what it meant—'BTW a FOAF tells me you are interested in joining us, GMTA'?

This chapter looks at these things and more. You'll learn about personalising your messages, using special stationery, automatic responses and alternative email services, as well as some other aspects of Internet email.

PERSONALISING YOUR MESSAGES

There are ways you can make your messages express your personality. These same methods can be used to make correspondence with outside customers reflect the company's image.

One way to quickly stamp a message with your style is to have an individual greeting and signature. Are you the type of person who greets people with 'Hi there, Fred' or 'Dear Fred', or 'Freddo'? Do you sign off with 'Cheers' or 'Regards' or 'Bye for now'? Develop a way to greet and sign off that is reflective of you and the way you speak.

A longer signature gives you more room to be creative. Some people draw pictures using keyboard characters, like in the example below.

▨ A picture signature

```
@..@        Fran Foster
(\—/)       f_foster@aaaint.com.au
(.>__<.)    16 Wealth Street, Melbourne
^^^ ^^^     Ph 03 0000 0000
```

There are many examples of this art. However, pictures like this only work well with fixed-width (typewriter-style) fonts. To a person displaying the message using a proportional font it's likely to appear squashed or unrecognisable, so it can be a risk unless you know that the people you are dealing with will pick up the fixed-font setting. Also, with more modern graphical options now available, these pictures can look dated unless they are very clever.

> *I have a friend who includes a link to the local weather forecast in his signature. This is a cheerful reminder that he lives in the sunshine while I'm enduring the winter cold.*
>
> —*Roberto, Office Worker*

People often include a link to their personal World Wide Web page or favourite Web site. Another option is to include a pithy saying or quote that interests or inspires you.

▨ A signature with a quote

Narelle Fischer
n_fischer@aaaint.com.au

'Whether you think you can or think you can't - you are right.'
- Henry Ford

For a formal business message you might include the company slogan in this way. Whatever you choose to do, don't make your signature so long that it overpowers your message.

AUTOMATING YOUR SIGNATURE

You won't want to be typing a multi-line signature each time you send a message. This is where an automatic signature is helpful. Look for options on your mailer which allow you to type and save the text of your signature and link it to your messages. Now when you type messages you don't type a signature—the signature you created is automatically inserted at the end of each message.

It's an added advantage if your mailer allows you to create multiple signatures. This lets you have one for formal business, another for colleagues and a third for close friends. Alternatively, you could use a form letter for this purpose.

If you don't want to go to the trouble of having multiple signatures, or your mailer doesn't have a method for you to do it, then you should opt for a signature that will suit both business and personal correspondence. It can be individual without being too quirky and personal.

USING AN ELECTRONIC BUSINESS CARD

If your mailer has the vCard facility, you can add an electronic business card. vCard is a special format for recording business card details. Mailers and other computer programs which understand the vCard format can read the business card and load it into their address book. It's a quick way to supply people with all of the addressing information you would like them to have, such as your company name, title, street address, telephone and fax numbers, and World Wide Web home page.

A mailer which supports this facility will have a way for you to type your business card details and create a vCard file. You can then set up the mailer to automatically attach this file to your email messages. It will also have a way of showing you when a message you receive has a business card attached, so you can click on it to load the details directly into your address book.

INSERTING CLICKABLE LINKS

Modern mailers will automatically detect World Wide Web addresses and email addresses and make these clickable links. Clickable links are displayed as underlined text. They are also known as *hyperlinks* or *hot links*.

Clicking on a clickable email address opens a new message to send to that address. Clicking on a clickable Web address automatically loads the Web browser and goes to the specified page.

Some mailers allow you to create clickable links from other text and graphics as well. For example, you could write a message which says 'To find out more, click here'. In this case 'here' is a clickable link to a Web site where there is more information on the topic.

To create a link like this, you usually select the text with your cursor and then select the 'Make hyperlink' option. A dialogue box appears asking you to supply the Web address you want connected with the text. A Web address is also called a *URL* (Uniform Resource Locater).

To use this option you need to be sure the recipient has a mailer that recognises Web links, otherwise you are better off spelling out the Web address so they can access it manually.

USING HTML STATIONERY

Some mailers allow you to create stationery in HTML format. *HTML* (HyperText Markup Language) is the authoring

> *I hate people sending large email messages containing unnecessary graphics when simple text would suffice.*
>
> —*Nandini, Business Analyst*

language used in creating World Wide Web pages. You will need someone who understands HTML to create the stationery file for you. You then save it in the disk directory or folder where the mailer looks for stationery.

If you are familiar with the World Wide Web you will realise that you can create highly graphic layouts with HTML. You will also know that a Web page with a lot of images and multimedia effects can take a very long time to load. So, while your mailer may allow you to create and use very graphic stationery it's often not a good idea. A person on a slow link will not be impressed at the amount of time it takes to load your message only to find it contains a short paragraph overlaid on a complex picture. On the other hand, using a small company logo to create an attractive business letterhead may be a good idea (see Figure 8.1).

What you must understand is that people outside your company may not be using a mailer that is as sophisticated as yours. Some mailers will not be able to display HTML-format messages. If you send a message in HTML format to a mailer which can't handle it, it may display as plain text with an HTML attachment that can be viewed using a World Wide Web browser. People who don't understand what is going on will find this confusing. Worse still, it may display with HTML commands embedded in the text. This isn't very friendly and is quite unlike the professional image you are trying to convey.

If you know the recipients can't handle HTML stationery, then use an alternative plain text letterhead. Your mailer should also allow you to send an HTML message in plain text format. If you are careful in your design, this may create

Figure 8.1 Letterhead using a company logo

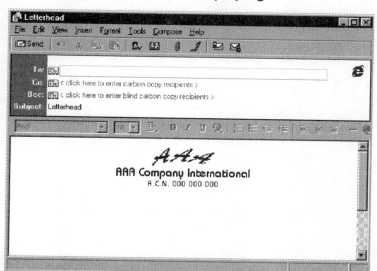

an acceptable result. The earlier HTML letterhead would appear as in Figure 8.2.

Your address book may allow you to indicate whether the person's mailer uses HTML or plain text. When you are using HTML stationery and don't know what type of mailer the recipient has, use plain text format.

USING AUTOMATIC FORWARDING AND REPLIES

The ability to send an automated response to all incoming messages is available with many corporate email systems. The most common use for this is to inform people that you aren't in the office so they know you won't answer your email messages quickly. The message in the automated response may

Figure 8.2 Letterhead in plain text

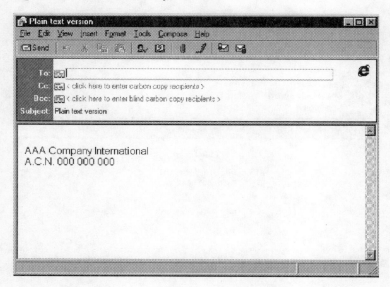

be something like in the example below. This message will go to everyone who sends a message to you.

An automated response message

I am on leave until 10 August. For assistance while I'm away, please contact Diana Sim.

When you return, remove the message. It's easy to forget because you don't see the message. At the time you set it up, it's a good idea to send yourself a reminder message and leave it in your inbox to read when you get back.

While you are away you may need another person to handle your mail. You won't want to give them full access to your mailer. Fortunately, there is usually a way around this with corporate email systems. You can automatically forward all of your incoming email to the person doing your job. At the time you set up the automatic forwarding you may also be given the option of deleting the messages from your inbox when you forward them or keeping a copy for yourself to read on your return.

Automatic redirection is also helpful for forwarding email to an alternative email address—your home address, for example.

If you are using an email account through a service provider, these functions work

I don't mind 'I'm away' notices, but getting something useless like 'Thank you for your message' every time I write to a person is annoying. I also hate getting 'I'm away' messages weeks after the person has come back.

—Simon, Administrative Assistant

I always have my email forwarded to my secretary as well as keeping a copy for myself. She handles my appointments and the routine items and knows where to find me if something is urgent.

—Rebecca, Business Executive

differently. While your mailer may have the ability to send an automatic response or to redirect all messages, these usually work as the messages are read into your inbox. You will have to leave your computer set up to automatically connect to the server on a regular basis to read and redirect the messages. An alternative is to see if your service provider will temporarily redirect messages to another account while you are away.

USING ALTERNATIVE EMAIL SERVICES

If you receive a lot of personal email, you should consider having a personal email account. Also, when you are on business trips it can be difficult to access your office email without incurring costly long-distance telephone calls. Having a personal email account can help you to get around this problem too. Here are some ideas for you to consider.

A personal ISP account can provide better access

One way to get a personal email account is to arrange for a connection with an *Internet Service Provider (ISP)*. This will give you Internet access and a personal email address.

Before you go away, get your office mailer to redirect all incoming messages to your personal email address. You can then read the messages from this account and send your replies. If you plan to travel far, choose your ISP carefully.

A problem is that when you send work-related messages from your personal account it will have your personal email address as the reply address and this may confuse people. Some mailers let you specify a different reply-to address than the one from which the email message is sent. If your mailer has this facility, then set the reply-to address as your normal office email address. Otherwise, include in your signature something like this:

▓ A message directing people to reply as you want

This message has been sent from a temporary address.
Please reply to n_fischer@aaaint.com.au

Free email is another way

Another alternative for out-of-office access is free email. There are several providers of free email on the Internet. To obtain a free email account you have to give the provider varying amounts of personal information which can be used to target you with advertising. They fund the free service through advertising. In return you get an email address

> I chose an ISP which has access points all over the world. Now when I'm away I can usually handle my email with just a local phone call even if I'm in another country
>
> —*Cordelia, Sales Manager*

which is usually quite func-
tional and easy to use, but
access can be slow at times.

To access free email you
go to the provider's World
Wide Web site which gives
you access to a mailer and
your messages. The mailer
usually works with a Web-
based browser. This means
you don't need email software
loaded on the computer you are using.

> *My daughter obtained a free
> email account through her school.
> I was surprised when we were vis-
> iting a museum in another city
> that she could read her email
> using their Internet computer.
> I realised this was something
> that could help me when I was
> travelling.*
>
> —*Martin, Business Executive*

Before you leave home you redirect your mail to your free
email address. You can access the free email site (and hence
your messages) from any computer connected to the World
Wide Web. With Internet access readily available in most
cities, at places like libraries, businesses and Internet cafes,
this is an ideal way to be able to process your email when
you are away from home.

Messages sent from the free email site may have some
form of advertising about the site attached to them, so if
you're sending work messages remember to include your own
message telling people your normal office address as in the
earlier example.

You will need to handle multiple accounts

If you are going to use your work computer to access a
personal ISP account, you are going to need to set it up to
handle multiple connections—one connection to your office
email and another to your personal email account. If your
mailer is unable to handle multiple accounts, you will need
two mailers.

Be aware that your company may not like you using your
work computer for outside email services because it could

bypass the normal virus-checking mechanisms they have established. They may also be concerned about the security risk of confidential messages being sent outside the company. If you are in doubt, check the company's policy or ask your email administrator.

UNDERSTANDING INTERNET MAIL PROTOCOLS

If you get involved with establishing a personal email account on the Internet, you will come across references to mail protocols such as SMTP and POP3. You can get by without understanding them other than knowing that successful communication requires both computers to use the same protocols. They are briefly explained here in case you are wondering what they are all about.

What is a mail protocol?

Mail protocols are agreed procedures used by computers to allow messages to be transferred successfully.

Proprietary protocols are those which belong to a specific computer company. It's usually either difficult or expensive to make computers using different proprietary protocols talk together. It's a bit like one person talking Chinese and the other Spanish, with no translator. This is why standard protocols such as SMTP are agreed between different computer companies so that they 'talk the same language'.

There are many different standard protocols used in relation to email for different tasks. Here are some that you will come across for Internet email. Corporate email systems may use proprietary protocols rather than these.

Some standard protocols

SMTP (Simple Mail Transfer Protocol) is the mail protocol used for transferring email messages between email servers on the

Internet. It's also the protocol used to send messages from the mailer to the Internet email server.

POP (Post Office Protocol) is the most commonly used protocol for Internet mailers to retrieve messages from an email server. The current version is POP3. Mailers which use POP3 allow you to work offline. Once you have collected your new messages, you can disconnect the line and read and process your mail. When you are ready to send messages, you can reconnect the line and send them. Mailers which use POP3 usually delete the email messages from the server once they have been successfully retrieved from the server. The messages and folders are kept on the desktop computer.

IMAP (Internet Message Access Protocol) is a newer protocol, similar to POP3, which is used by the mailer to retrieve messages from the email server. The current version is IMAP4. IMAP has some extra features that allow you to keep and work with messages while they are still on the server.

> The Internet mailer I use with my personal account has IMAP4, S/MIME and LDAP and can handle HTML stationery. This gives it all of the latest features and is easy to use.
>
> —Matt, Research Assistant

MIME (Multipurpose Internet Mail Extension) is a mail transfer protocol that encodes multimedia attachments to allow them to be transferred with messages.

S/MIME (Secure/MIME) adds digital signatures and encryption to the MIME protocol. This is a new protocol that has not yet been fully agreed as a standard.

LDAP (Lightweight Directory Access Protocol) is a set of protocols that allow address book information, like email addresses and public encryption keys, to be easily shared by different computer programs. It also lets your mailer look up public databases of addresses that are stored in LDAP format.

DEMYSTIFYING EMAIL JARGON

Over the years an email culture has emerged which has its own language and way of doing things. For example, *abbreviations* or acronyms are used to reduce keystrokes. In business most of this jargon is either not understood or avoided. However, you may see some of the terms slipping in among the group of people you deal with. Here is some of the more common email jargon.

BTW	By the way
F2F	Face to face
FAQ	Frequently asked question
FOAF	Friend of a friend
FYA	For your action (sometimes For your amusement)
FYI	For your information
FWIW	For what it's worth
GMTA	Great minds think alike
IMHO	In my humble opinion
IRL	In real life
ROTFL	Rolling on the floor laughing
TTFN	Ta-ta for now
TIA	Thanks in advance
TNX	Thanks
TTYL	Talk to you later
WTG	Way to go
YMMV	Your mileage may vary (a disclaimer)

Flaming is sending inflammatory remarks or messages as an email attack. If you upset people on Internet mailing lists, you are likely to be flamed in return. When flames go back and forth this is known as a *flame war*.

List server is an automatic mailing list server for Internet mailing lists (email discussion groups). There is more on this in the next chapter.

Netiquette is the rules of good manners on the Internet, particularly in Internet discussion groups. Many of the ideas presented in this book explain the netiquette of email. The next chapter has the special netiquette considerations for email discussion groups.

Net saints are experienced users who are prepared to share their knowledge with newcomers. Look for net saints to help you.

Newbies are new users on the Internet. Newbies to discussion groups should go carefully until they know the culture of the group, otherwise they run the risk of being flamed.

Newsgroups are online discussion groups similar to Internet mailing lists but they don't use email. You may need a newsreader in addition to your mailer to read and send messages to newsgroups.

Posting is publishing a message in a discussion group such as an Internet mailing list or newsgroup.

Punctuation uses have emerged to compensate for mailers not being able to display bold, italic and such. Here are some you might see for emphasising words.

word	Word in italics
word	Underlined word
WORD	Strong emphasis

Shouting is writing messages all in CAPITAL LETTERS. It's rude to shout for more than a few words.

Snail mail is paper-based mail sent through the ordinary mail system. It is called this because it is so slow in comparison to email.

Smileys, also called *emoticons*, are pictures of facial expressions created using various character combinations. They are viewed sideways—for example, :-) is a smiley face. Their aim is to convey the emotion behind the words. To show something is a joke, for example, you could attach a smiley. There are hundreds of these and not all people interpret them the same way.

Spam is unwanted unsolicited email and is also called electronic junk mail. Spammers send their messages to any email address they can obtain.

CONNECTING TO THE WORLD WITH INTERNET EMAIL

The Internet has evolved into a powerful worldwide communication network that lets you send and receive email with ease anywhere in the world. The Internet is also a friendly place where you can meet people with similar interests.

The next chapter introduces you to the friendly aspects of email, including how to join discussion groups through Internet mailing lists.

KEY POINTS

- Personalise your messages with:
  - Your greeting.
  - Your signature.
  - A small picture or logo, a quote or a Web link.
  - HTML stationery.
  - Your business card.
- Manage your email while you are away by:
  - Sending an automatic message telling people you are out.
  - Forwarding your messages to someone else.
  - Forwarding your messages to an alternative email account that you can access more easily.
  - Only use email jargon when it is common practice in the group you are corresponding with.

EXERCISES

Complete these exercises to learn how to use some of the features described in this chapter.

1. **Look at the different personal signatures that people use and decide which approaches you like.**
   Without stealing someone else's idea, design your own signature. (If you already have a personal signature, it's a good idea to revamp it occasionally to keep it fresh.)

2. **If your mailer has the capability, create an electronic business card and attach it to an email message.**

chapter 9

Is it really possible to enjoy email?

Email can be fun to receive and fun to write. Throughout this book you have been learning how to get through the business of email efficiently. One of the good things about doing this is that it gives you time to relax and enjoy yourself. Humour and friendship help the hassles of the day pass by more easily.

This chapter looks at email friendships both inside and outside your company. If your email system has access to the Internet, you will find it's a great way to renew old friendships and to find new acquaintances. It's not surprising that email is the most widely used application on the Internet today.

KEEPING IN TOUCH WITH FRIENDS AND FAMILY

Most people have some friends and family that live at a distance, that they rarely call and even less often write to. Email is a pleasant way to keep contact and won't add too many extra messages to your inbox.

Be spontaneous

A short email message sent once in a while is much less effort than writing a letter. Letters seem to beg for the page to be filled and then require you to find a postage stamp and remember to drop it in the post box. A brief, chatty and topical email message can be dashed off in a few minutes and sent on its way.

You can base your correspondence on a regular exchange of messages (you write, then I write, then you write and so on), in much the same way as letters. However, email also has the flexibility to be much more spontaneous as well.

> *When my nieces do something cute or funny, it's not worth a letter and usually gets forgotten by the time we talk on the phone. My sister pops the story into an email message and I enjoy getting the unexpected laugh.*
>
> —*Norma, Adoring Aunt*

How often should you write?

There is an interesting dilemma when your friendship is based on email exchanges. People who write letters don't expect a reply for a month or two. When people send email messages they tend to hope for a reply very quickly.

If you reply quickly, then you either find yourself sending too many messages for comfort or you're always putting the onus on the other person to initiate the next round.

The other side of the problem is, if you wait a month or two the other person may think their message didn't arrive. Perhaps the solution is to send a quick reply saying something like this, 'I enjoyed your note. I'll write later' until a pattern of delay has been established.

Include pictures

If you have access to a scanner, then you have another way to brighten your correspondence. Getting copies of photographs can be a nuisance, and remembering to post them is a problem too. A scanner saves you the trouble. Scan and attach that photo of the new boat or the big catch or the kids in fancy dress. It'll be appreciated.

MAKING NEW FRIENDS THROUGH INTERNET MAILING LISTS

In addition to fostering old friendships, email can help you to find new friends. There are tens of thousands of email mailing lists, some of which may cover your work interests or hobbies.

Types of Internet mailing lists

An Internet mailing list is a group of people who have a shared interest which they discuss via email. There are different styles to these mailing lists, depending on how they are managed, the size of the group and their reason for existence.

With *discussion lists* the people in the group participate in a discussion. Email messages are sent to everyone in the group and anyone in the group joins the discussion by replying or starting a new topic of discussion (provided it is within the sphere of interest of the group).

Other lists operate as *announcement lists* where a central coordinator sends regular

> *I'm on a discussion list that covers my specialist area. I've found it useful for getting help and opinions about the things I'm trying to do. I get ideas from the discussion and can help others too.*
>
> —*Nicolas, Systems Programmer*

.notices or newsletters to the members of the group. The members are informed by these but don't take part in a discussion, except perhaps through a submission to the editor.

Many of the lists are *private lists* which are restricted to a particular group of people. They might, for example, be members of a club or professional association. There are a growing number of groups like this.

> *Receiving government press releases gives me access to the latest political information very quickly.*
>
> —*Adrian, Economist*
>
> ---
>
> *We decided to replace our printed newsletter with an email mailing list to help us cut costs. We only make it available to paid-up members of our association.*
>
> —*Lorrain, Non-profit Organisation*

Some of these lists will require you to present your credentials before allowing you to join. There are, however, plenty of *public lists* which have no restriction on membership.

Some of the discussion lists are *moderated lists*, which means that you submit your replies and discussion topics to the moderator rather than posting them directly to the group. The moderator decides on the suitability of your message and may edit it before it goes out to the group. Moderating a list keeps the group on topic. *Unmoderated lists* allow any member of the group to post messages to the group as a whole. The people in the group will generally keep the topics on track by objecting to unsuitable postings.

Some mailing lists produce a *digest*. Instead of you receiving a new message in your mailbox each time someone posts an item, the messages are bundled together and sent out periodically. A digest may be sent each day or when a certain number of messages have been received.

Find a list

There are several ways of finding suitable lists to join. You can ask colleagues, friends and family what lists they have found to be useful and interesting.

> When searching the Web I found a page on International Law with information about a mailing list. It's my area of my research, so I joined up.
>
> —Mark, Research Student

There is no one place that has the names of all of the lists, but there are some World Wide Web sites that have gathered information on a lot of them. The sites 'http://www.liszt.com' and 'http://www.reference.com' are good places to start.

Many of the lists may seem suitable but may in fact be private, or the coverage of the topic is too broad, too academic or otherwise not of interest to you. It's a good idea to do your research and find out as much as you can about the group—from the directories, home pages or friends—before you join. Some lists have *archives* of past discussions which you can access. These will give you a good idea about how the group operates.

JOINING AND LEAVING INTERNET MAILING LISTS

Joining a list is called *subscribing*. Most mailing lists are managed automatically by a *mailing list server*.

Join a list by subscribing

To subscribe to a list, you have to send an email message to the server with a special command in the body of the message. The mailing list server will have two addresses, an administration address (where you send subscription requests and

Figure 9.1 Subscribing to an Internet mailing list

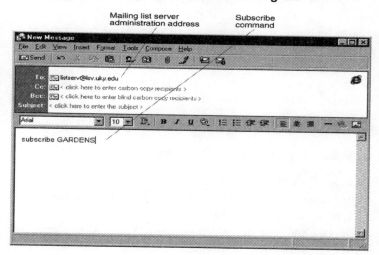

other commands) and a listname address (which you use to post messages to the group). Make sure you send your subscription request to the administration address. The way you join will be something like the example given in Figure 9.1, which is subscribing to the 'GARDENS' list.

You must follow the special instructions for the list you are joining. You are usually writing to a computer which is often managing more than one list, so you must get the name exactly right to be successfully added to the list. Also, turn off your signature file. Otherwise it may try to interpret the lines of your signature and get errors.

If you are subscribing to a list from a group's World Wide Web page, you may only have to complete the details on the page and it will do the subscribing for you.

When you are successfully subscribed to the list you will usually receive a welcome message. *Keep your welcome message.* It will tell you information about the group and how to unsubscribe from the list, as well as other basic commands you can use. For example, if the list runs a digest version you should be given the command to change your subscription to digest.

Most lists will only accept postings from subscribed members. If you want to participate from two different email addresses, then you need to subscribe for each of these addresses.

Unsubscribe to leave the group

You may find the list doesn't suit you or is sending too many messages. Your welcome message should give you information on how to unsubscribe from the list. Usually it's as simple as sending a message to the administration address with the words 'unsubscribe listname'. Messages may still come through for a day or two after you unsubscribe and will then stop.

Most servers will only accept commands sent from the email address of a subscribed member. If you are going to change your email address, remember to unsubscribe before you finish with your old address and then subscribe again from your new address.

Some list servers will also have commands that you can issue to stop mail and resume mail. This is useful to stop the flow of mail when you are going away for a while.

Try it, it's not hard

Even though there appear to be a lot of instructions here, you will find that joining Internet mailing lists isn't difficult. Basically you find a list which interests you, you subscribe to it and keep the welcome message so that you can unsubscribe later. It's worth seeing if there's a group that suits you and giving it a try.

HANDLING INTERNET MAILING LIST DISCUSSIONS

Soon after you subscribe, you should begin receiving email messages that are posted to the group. The number of messages you receive will depend on how active the discussion is.

Organise the messages

Messages from mailing lists are usually less important than your normal work and you don't want them cluttering your inbox. So remember to get yourself organised. Make a folder for each of the lists you join and if possible set up a filter so the messages are automatically put in the folders.

The filter will be easy as messages coming from the mailing list server will have the same address each time. When you get your first message, set up a filter to file messages coming from that address.

Join the discussion

When you have something to offer to the discussion, share it. It's the participants, not the watchers, who make the groups function. To participate in the discussion you simply reply to one of the postings. This will open a message addressed to the whole list not just to the person who posted the original message. Leave the subject unchanged so members can follow the conversation thread.

The list server may not waste resources by sending you a copy of your posting, so if you want to know what you wrote keep a copy when you send it.

Follow the netiquette

Every group will have their own rules and way of behaving. Here are some general guidelines for mailing list netiquette to help you get started smoothly.

Wait for a couple of weeks and watch the discussion before posting anything yourself. Some groups have a strong sense of community, and you don't want to barge in as an interloper. In a few weeks you will know the right way to introduce yourself and participate.

Follow the rules for posting new messages. Some groups have conventions which they follow, like including 'Help' or 'Answer' in the subject line to help people sort their messages more quickly. There may be instructions on this in your welcome message. Otherwise, watch what other people do.

Use the FAQs (Frequently Asked Questions) and archives when they are provided to find out more about the group and to save asking questions that have been discussed before.

Use plain text because it will be compatible with all of the contributors to the group.

Only reply to the group as a whole if it will interest them. If your answer won't interest everyone, reply directly to the original contributor. To do this, compose a new message and type in their address; don't use the reply option.

Include a minimum of context. To keep the traffic to a minimum, don't include the whole message that you are replying to as context. However, include enough to make your message clear.

Keep your signature short. Long, complicated signatures are frowned on by some groups.

Keep to the topic. Group members have joined the list to follow particular topics. Going off on a tangent outside the charter of the group won't be appreciated.

Don't post advertisements. Most group members don't want advertisements of any kind. If you post an advertisement, even though it may seem of interest to the people in the group, you may be banned from the group. If you think you have something of interest that may be construed as an advertisement, ask the owner who manages the list before you post the item.

Remember that lists are often archived. What you post could be available for a very long time, so don't say something that might come back and haunt you.

Consider your company

If you are using your work email address, then you must be careful that the personal thoughts in your postings are not construed as the opinion of your company. You should include a disclaimer.

▓ Disclaimer for mailing list postings

These opinions are my own and do not necessarily represent the opinion of AAA Company International.

Even with such a disclaimer, people may view your messages as having some validity from your company. This is particularly the case if the discussion is in close association with the work done by your company.

For example, if you have joined a discussion group about gardening and you work for an accounting firm, then your views are unlikely to be seen as your company's perspective on the topic. If, however, you work for a large plant nursery, then your opinion takes on a different value, despite any disclaimers you may use. If there is a risk of this problem, you should obtain and use a personal email account for contributing to the list.

AVOIDING SPAM CAUSED BY INTERNET MAILING LISTS

When you subscribe to an Internet mailing list, you will almost certainly attract some spam (unsolicited advertising material). A favourite pastime of spammers is to subscribe to lists to gain access to the addresses of the participants.

Here are some possible ways of keeping your address from spammers. The alternative to keeping your address from spammers is to handle the spam when it arrives using the ideas given in Chapter 4.

Get off the subscribed members list

The mailing list servers keep a list of all of the subscribed members and their addresses. In some cases, members (including spammers) can display this list. One way to protect your address is to get it off this list. See if your welcome letter tells you how to do this.

Alter your email address

Even if your name is hidden in the subscriber list, the spammer's computer programs may still pick up your address from any discussion postings that you make. If your mailer lets you specify the reply-to address, you can alter this in a way to trick their computer software programs.

▧ Changing the reply-to address to avoid spam

Real address:	'j_noakes@aaaint.com.au'
Reply-to address:	'j_noakes@antispam.aaaint.com.au'

The spammer's email messages will be sent to an address which doesn't exist, while people replying to you will know to remove 'antispam' from your address before they send it. You can do the same with your signature file or remove your email address from your signature file when posting to lists.

Use an anonymous remailer

It's also possible to use an anonymous remailer. You send your message to an anonymous remailer which sends it on with a different address, thus hiding your identity. You will find addresses for anonymous remailers on the World Wide Web.

WORKING WITH A SMILE

There have been lots of tips and hints in this book to help you to overcome the burden of email—things like organising yourself, ignoring the chit-chat, keeping your messages short and not copying people unnecessarily. Hopefully, you have taken on the challenge and acted on at least a few of the ideas. If so, you should be already feeling the difference. Now it's time to relax the rules.

Give your messages a personal touch occasionally

That chit-chat which is superfluous can also be heart-warming. People like to know that you think of them as friends, not just as a means of getting your job done. Slip in something that shows you have thought of them. Is it their birthday or some other special milestone? Has their team won? Do you have a snippet of news to share?

Don't overdo it but try it sometimes, even for the people you are less inclined to like. It works wonders.

Go ahead, be funny once in a while

When you read someone's message and a witty reply pops into your head, go ahead and type it. It will only take a second or two and will put a smile on another face. A light-hearted response every once in a while is refreshing. A whimsical touch in your signature file can also brighten someone's day.

Say thank you every now and then

Generally you don't send a reply saying 'Thank you'. It's a waste of everyone's time. When someone has really gone out of their way to be helpful, or has been consistently helpful for a long time, then waste their time and make their day. Say 'Thank you, I really appreciate your good work' and copy their boss as well.

Have a frivolous conversation sometimes

Even indulge in an entirely frivolous conversation sometimes. Playfulness bonds people together and makes a team successful. Email, with its conversational style, makes this easy and fun.

ENJOY EMAIL

With a little bit of organisation and practice you can get on top of your email and give yourself time to be happy and friendly. When you smile, the people around you smile.

Enjoy your email and others will enjoy it with you.

KEY POINTS

- Keep in touch with friends and family by:
  — Sending spontaneous messages that include a picture or two.
  — Exchanging messages not so frequently that it's a burden.
- When joining an Internet mailing list:
  — Subscribe to a list which interests you and organise the incoming messages so they don't interfere with your work.
  — Keep your welcome letter so that you know how to leave the group.

- — If it's an interactive group, take part in the discussion, keeping to the rules and customs of the group.
- — Consider whether you should use a personal email address rather than your company email address and take action to keep your address from advertisers.
- Make your messages friendly by:
  - — Giving them a personal touch occasionally.
  - — Using humour once in a while.
  - — Remembering every now and then to thank the people who help you.
  - — Enjoying your email.

EXERCISES

Use these exercises to start making email friends. Exercises 1 and 2 only apply if you are able to send and receive mail on the Internet.

1. **Do you have friends and family who have Internet email addresses?**
   More and more people are getting email connections each day. Start collecting their addresses and put them in your address book. Send them a note to let them know your address and take it from there.

2. **Ask colleagues whether there is an Internet mailing list that will be valuable for you to join. Subscribe to it.**

3. **Add a personal touch, a sense of humour, or say thanks in at least one email message today.**

Email basics

There are some basic things you need to know to begin sending and receiving email messages. The software that you run to read and send email messages is called a *mailer*. (It is also known as an *email application* or an *email client*.)

Because there are many different mailers, it's not possible to give you specific instructions on how to use your particular one. You will need help from a manual, the online help facility, or a person in your office who knows how your mailer works. What is given here are some general instructions that show you the things you should be able to do with your mailer.

These general instructions assume you are dealing with a graphical mailer which uses a mouse to select items from menus and to click on icons. You may have a command-driven mailer which requires you to type commands instead. Either way, use this appendix to find out what you need to know and set about finding out how to do it with your mailer.

STARTING YOUR MAILER

You start your mailer the same way as you start other applications on your computer. You usually click on its icon or

Figure A.1 A message list

List of messages
in the inbox

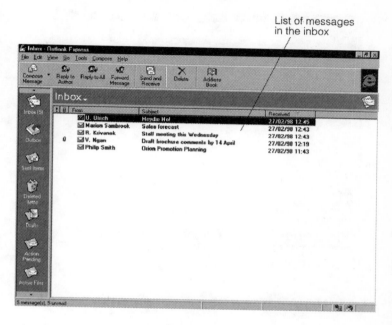

select it from the program menu. If your email is accessed through a service provider, you will need to dial the provider and connect to their computer as well as starting your mailer. The mailer may do this automatically for you.

VIEWING THE LIST OF RECEIVED MESSAGES

When you start your mailer it will display a list of the messages that you have received. You may have to open the inbox (by clicking on the inbox icon) to get this. The list of incoming messages may look something like that shown in Figure A.1.

Some mailers will display the messages in a preview window as you move the selector down the list.

Figure A.2 An open message

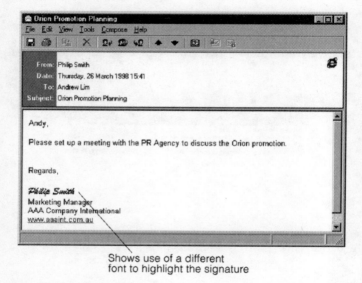

Shows use of a different
font to highlight the signature

READING A MESSAGE

To read a particular message in the list, you select the message
and issue the read command (by double clicking on the
message or selecting 'Read' or 'Open' from the menu bar).
The message will be opened and displayed for you to read,
as shown in Figure A.2.

You close the message by closing its window.

REPLYING TO A MESSAGE

To reply to a message, select the message you want to reply
to and then select the 'Reply' command (from the menu bar).
This will open a new message addressed to the person who
sent you the original message and will be copied to any people
who were copied on the original message (see Figure A.3).

Figure A.3 A message opened for reply

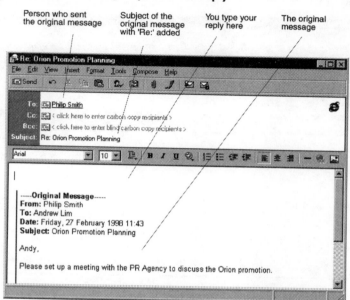

Person who sent
the original message

Subject of the
original message
with 'Re:' added

You type your
reply here

The original
message

Depending on how your mailer is set up, it may contain the text of the original message within the new message. Your mailer may also have an option to reply just to the sender of the original message and not to the other copied recipients.

Type your message. If you make a mistake when you are typing, you can use the normal keys for backspacing and deleting to correct the message. (This may be more complicated on a command-driven mailer.) When you have finished the message, send it using the 'Send' command (from the menu bar).

SENDING A NEW MESSAGE

Sometimes you will want to send a new message rather than just replying to an existing one. To compose a new message,

Figure A.4 A new message

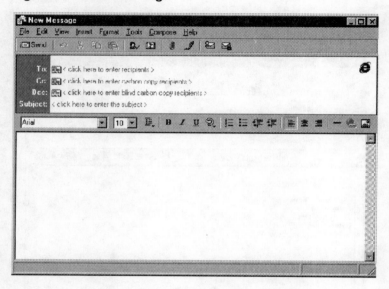

select the 'New message' command (from the menu bar). This will open a new empty message, as shown in Figure A.4.

Type the addresses of the people who are to receive your message in the 'To:' and 'Cc:' fields. Also type a subject and the body of your message. When you have finished writing your message, send it using the 'Send' command.

FINDING ADDRESSES

If you work on a corporate email system, addresses of people in your company are probably stored in an address book which you can access with your mailer. Typing the first few letters of a person's name will often display the rest of the address without you having to type it all. It may give you a selection list when the name matches several names. With some mailers you may have to open the address book and select names from there.

For names that are not in the address book, you have to type the address exactly as you have been given it, from a business card, letterhead or some other source.

PRINTING A MESSAGE

You can print the message that is displayed using the 'Print' command (from the menu bar). This will display the normal print dialogue box from which you can select which printer to use.

DELETING A MESSAGE

To delete a message, you select the message and use the 'Delete' command (from the menu bar, or you may be able to drag-and-drop the message on to a trash icon). Deleting a message often does not delete the message permanently until you clear the trash (an item on the menu bar).

PUTTING A MESSAGE IN A FOLDER

The messages will usually stay in the inbox until you either delete them or file them in a folder. Your mailer may allow you to create folders with names that suit you (follow the 'New folder' option on the menu bar). You can then move a message to a folder using the 'Move' or 'Transfer' command (from the menu bar, or you may be able to drag-and-drop the message into the folder).

To see the messages you have stored in a folder, you open the folder (click on the folder or use the menu bar).

ATTACHING A DOCUMENT TO A MESSAGE

To attach a document to a message, there may be a menu item for attaching the file. Select this and then follow the normal file selection dialogue boxes to choose the file you want to attach. If there is no menu item, the method for attaching documents will be more complicated. You will need to follow the instructions in your documentation.

EXITING FROM THE MAILER

Close the mailer by closing its window or issuing the 'Exit' command (from the menu bar).

OTHER THINGS TO KNOW

There are other things you should know which are covered in some detail in this book. These include:

- creating and using personal address book entries
- addressing a lot of people at once with mail groups
- searching for messages
- using filters to automatically file and respond to messages
- automatic forwarding and replying
- creating forms, templates and stationery
- creating automatic signatures.

PRACTISE BY SENDING MESSAGES TO YOURSELF

Learn how to use your mailer by sending some messages to yourself. Do this by creating a new message, typing your own address and sending it. Send yourself several messages. They will appear in your inbox. (You may need to issue a command to read new messages for them to be delivered.) You can now practise reading, printing, filing and deleting messages.

Once you begin to feel comfortable with your mailer, read the rest of this book, to learn how to be an effective email user.